how2become

a Game Designer

The ultimate guide
to breaking into
the game industry

Joshua Brown

Orders: Please contact How2become Ltd, Suite 3, 50 Churchill Square Business Centre, Kings Hill, Kent ME19 4YU. You can also order via the e-mail address info@how2become.co.uk.

ISBN: 9781909229617

CONTENTS

PREFACE

This book has been written with the intention to help any aspiring video game entrepreneur get a job within the game industry. It is not necessary for you to know the specific area within the industry you wish to pursue- as this book covers, as best it can, the majority of roles and how to get you your dream job working in that role.

I began writing this book, to not only help people successfully obtain a career within the games industry, but also as it is a topic and an area of my life that I have a strong passion and enjoyment in. Within the game industry I work as a 3D artist. After going through the process of getting a job many times within the industry, I fully understand how much of a difficult process it can be.

Early on in my career I obtained a BA (hons) degree in 3D Modelling and Animation for Computer Games at the University of Derby. Since then I have worked for many different companies and I have helped many people achieve a job within the game industry.

 how2become

My book contains details on all the major roles within a game development studio, what their requirements are, sample interview questions, CVs, how to build your portfolio, working freelance and even setting up your own independent studio – all areas I have experience in.

I've thoroughly enjoyed writing my book and I hope that you get as much enjoyment in reading it.

Note: In this book, when I reference the term game designer, I am not referring to a specific role within the games industry, but rather I am using it to describe someone who creates, designs or has an input towards the development of a video game.

CHAPTER ONE

INTRODUCTION

WHAT IS A GAME?

Games are all around us, children play chase in the playground, adults may play a game of pool at their local pub, a game of cards at home or indeed video/computer games. The video game sector is the biggest within the entertainment industry. Films, TV and music all come second best compared to the global scale and success of the computer games industry. With blockbuster hits such as *Rockstar's Grand Theft Auto V* making over $1 Billion in its first month, and the surge in independent studios, there has never been a better time to join the video game industry.

Before I explain how you can get into this industry with ultimate insider tips and guidance, let us take a look at what it is to play video games and what it is to design them:

The official definition of a game is *"a contest, physical or mental, abiding to certain rules, recreation, or winning state."*

Game Player – Playing a game involves creating, testing and revising strategies as well as the skills necessary for progressing within the game.

Game Designer – Similarly, a game designer's role in the development of a game requires them to create, test, plan the best method of approach in design, and have the skills necessary to develop the game (software, communication skills etc).

So you enjoy playing computer games? You could say you have a passion for them? Well then you are already partially qualified to go out there and help make them.

Don't worry if you are uncertain as to how you want to help in the development of a game, as this will be covered later. This book will provide you with what you need to know to get the job of your choice within the game industry.

Now that you know what a game is and how this book will help you, it's time to crack on and learn what you need to to know to become a developer!

CHAPTER 2

THE STRUCTURE OF THE GAMES INDUSTRY

Before I begin to tell you the best methods and insider tips to becoming a games designer, it is important for you to have a strong understanding of the games industry itself and how it is structured. Although this does vary from studio to studio, there is a general structure for all game design. Let's start off by looking at where you will fit within the industry as a game designer.

Before you walk into any interview you should be aware of how the game industry is structured. Although you may not have interest in this 'non-creative' aspect, many things about the game industry only make sense if you know where the money comes from. Plus, any interviewer will be accustomed to thinking of the company's commercial enterprise, so the more you know about the industry, the better you will appear to them.

WHAT IS A DEVELOPER?

Developers and Publishers

Within the games industry, a game is created more often than not through a partnership between two different companies – a developer and a publisher. The developer (the company that you'll be working for as a games designer) is the company that will actually make the game through concepts, design, programming, art and audio etc. The publisher is often the company who provides funding, markets the game and then distributes it to your audience of gamers around the world.

It is worthwhile noting that there are three main types of relationships that a developer and a publisher may have:

- **A First Party Developer** – This is where the publisher entirely owns the developers. You will often see a particular game brand which is exclusive to a certain game system. In this case, it is most likely to have been developed by a first party developer.

- **Second Party Developers** – A second party developer is independent and therefore is not owned by a publisher. However, they will have a signed contract with a particular publisher that gives the publisher the exclusive right to publish their games.

- **Third Party Developer** – Third party developers mostly create games for multiple gaming platforms. This is by far the most common type of developer as it is seen as the best way to maximise profits by reaching the biggest audience possible. Third party developers sign their contracts with a publisher on a per-game basis.

The following diagram demonstrates the process a game makes from birth to finished product:

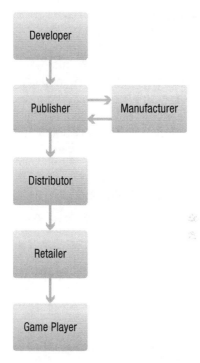

Who make up the video game audience?

The games you create in the industry will vary in terms of the demographic and who they are aimed for. However, it is worth considering that the average age for a gamer is around 30 years old, and of all gamers 49 per cent are females. This may surprise some, but it has been the reality for over a decade. Adults who grew up playing video games now want sophisticated, grown-up stories, which can sometimes be hard when games are not built on a story idea but rather enjoyment. The reality is the game industry is huge right now and there is opportunity to market games for anyone of any age or gender.

THE GAME DEVELOPMENT PIPELINE

Understanding the game development pipeline early on is a fantastic resource for any potential employer. It shows you have a good understanding of the industry you're entering and the quicker you'll be contributing to it. The game development pipeline is different to that of the game industry structure. The diagram below shows how the job roles within the game industry are typically structured in a hierarchy.

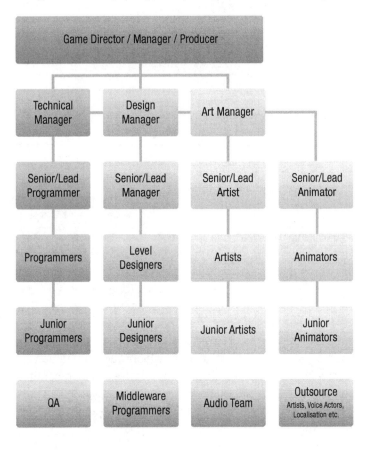

It is worth noting that the various roles at game studios do differ greatly. At one studio an animator may have a totally different set of tasks and duties to that of an animator at another studio. However in the following pages are descriptions that provide a general idea to what is available and what is expected in each role within the industry. This should then allow you to have a better understanding to what area you want to work in.

Although the following is perhaps viewed from an artistic perspective it provides a general idea to the pipeline of a games creation:

First, it is **DESIGNED**. Designers, including writers are the ones who create the origin for a game that you will eventually see on a store shelf. The ideas for the story and the game are passed onto the concept artists.

Secondly, **CONCEPTS** are made. A concept artist's job is to visually interpret the descriptions of the games world, ideas and characters from documents handed to them from the designers. Programmers will make early concept builds of the gameplay ideas.

Thirdly comes **MODELLING** – The modeller will then look at the art provided from the concepts and use that material to create 3D models or 2D models (depending on the games design). The art asset to be created could be the games character, vehicles or environment. 3D models are created using software such as *Autodesk's Maya* or *3D Studio Max*. The 3D artist will provide the art that will be used in the final game. However, before it does the work will be passed for texturing.

TEXTURE ARTISTS – The texture artist's role is to take the 3D/2D model and produce a texture for it. Textures

are primarily created within 2D programs such as Adobe Photoshop. Once again, the model is then moved on to another specialist.

RIGGING – The next step is to rig the model. The rigger's job is to make a model ready for animation. They do this by controlling the manipulable points of the 3D/2D model for animation. Rigging is often done by the animator themselves, or sometimes even a specialised modeller.

ANIMATION – The animator's job is to bring the static model to life, similar to how a puppeteer uses strings to put life into a wooden doll. The work of an animation artist is often referred to as Computer Generated Imagery (CGI).

VISUAL EFFECTS ARTIST – The work is then passed onto the Visual Effects (VFX) artist, whose role is to spice things up. They will generally do this by adding custom effects such as smoke, sparks or the character's footprints as they walk across the world. By adding this final polish the VFX artist really brings the 3D/2D object to a higher level of realism. This is the completion of the visual art pipeline.

AUDIO ARTIST – Furthermore, an audio artist will then produce the sound effects that match the 3D/2D object functions. They are also responsible for creating ambient noises and the background music.

PROGRAMMER – It is time for a programmer to get their hands on it. Although the programmers are involved throughout the games production, for the development of a game asset, this is where they may typically get involved. The programmer creates code to activate events, triggers and animations of 3D/2D model. Once this is done, it is given to a level designer.

LEVEL DESIGN – With level design, the 3D/2D object is

placed inside a game's level. It is a level designer's job to determine where to place objects to make it fun, fair and interesting for the game player.

QUALITY ASSURANCE (QA) – When working in the quality assurance department you will often be referred to as a QA tester. Under this title the QA tester is responsible for playing the game and hunting for bugs (unintentional errors found within the game). This information is then relayed back to the relevant department e.g. sound error will be reported to the audio team etc.

The majority of game development studios are made up of the kind of structure as described above although there can be further specialisation within the art, design and programming teams. Nowadays a lot of work is outsourced, particularly in 3D modelling, texturing and animation. This opens up the door to become a freelancer which will be covered more in a later chapter.

When starting off in the industry you will likely be presented with a junior role. It is a role that does hold limited responsibility and range but make the most of it as it does offer a gradual build up to your desired role and adds self-improvement and overall career progression.

PRODUCTION – WHO MAKE UP A DEVELOPMENT TEAM?

Once the development studio gets the go ahead to create a game, referred to as the green light, the project leaders will organise groups of individuals made up of the job roles mentioned briefly earlier. The development team will typically grow and shrink in areas throughout the project as shown in the diagram below:

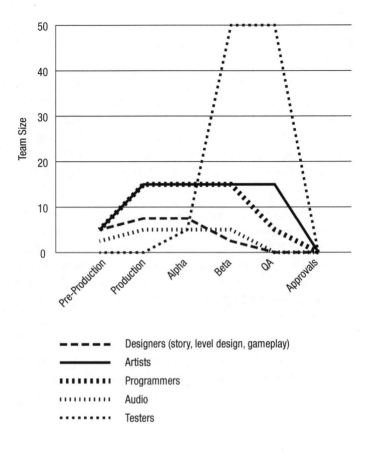

CHAPTER THREE

RESEARCHING AND
UNDERSTANDING YOUR ROLE

The best way to start, like most things, is to research. It's important for you to get a complete understanding of the jobs that interest you by learning their processes, skills and software/tools required for the game design role you're after. This section of the book will detail all of these requirements, provide example job listings and teach you how to research your chosen role to become an expert in its field.

Gather five or more of the job roles and their requirements and collate them together, from here you can see what you need to focus on at a personal level and an educational one.

The previous chapter described the roles within the games industry in a brief manner to give you a basic understanding of the roles available but this is not merely enough for you to know what it is for you to take on these roles.

DECIDING YOUR ROLE

Initially you may not know what area of games deign you will be best suited to. A good place to start is to ask yourself these questions:

"What do I enjoy about games?" – "Am I artistic?" – "Am I good at problem solving?" – "Do I enjoy making sure everything is in working order?" – "Am I good at programming?" – "Do I have a keen interest in sounds?"

It is not imperative that you know what route you want to take in the game industry just yet but having an idea of what you have a talent, appreciation and enjoyment for is a good way to setting yourself out on the right path. This chapter will provide an overview for all the different areas of game design and what it takes to become specialised in that area.

The following few pages will go in-depth into the various game designer roles.

PROGRAMMERS

What it is to be a Programmer

Programmers create a hub in which everything about the game revolves around. The software they create is the game. It is a hub that contains all the sounds files created by the audio team, the art assets from the art team, scripts, animation etc. As a programmer you will spend a lot of time writing code to create this 'hub' but you'll also be designing new routines and codes with artists, other programmers and the other teams in the studio. Although not necessarily creative in aesthetics it is a creative role because you as a programmer will have to use logic to create something robust and practical.

Skills and Requirements

To get a job as a games programmer you will need to be happy and content with mathematical concepts as all video games are in one way or another built upon maths. Different specialities within programming (graphical, physics, audio, artificial intelligence etc.) require a different amount of maths knowledge. As a programmer your starting rate of pay is higher than most in a development studio because you will already be expected to know your expertise. Before you apply for a programming job you should have already programmed a game of your own.

Example Software/Tools

Programming languages – There are many different programming languages but it is essential that you learn how to code using C++ as this is the main language used in game development.

GameMaker: Studio – GameMaker: Studio is a great tool for learning the basics of programming for games. The software

itself is a game engine and you should use it to create some simple games to develop your skills.

Application Programming Interfaces (APIs) – APIs are a set of pre-written software routines that you can incorporate into your games software to accomplish particular tasks. For example *Microsoft's DirectX* will give you the standard routines for programming graphics and other tasks so you, as the programmer, will not have to think of the actual hardware. OpenGL is another big player in the API sector and is worth learning.

Example Job Advert

Job Profile	*Junior Games Programmer*
Average Salary:	£22,000
Description:	Proficiency in programming and development for mobile/app based games is essential. You are required to have strong programming skills in C++ and Java. It is also desirable to have knowledge of *Epic's Unreal Game Engine*.
	For this role you will be reporting to the Senior Developer, working within a creative and fun team whose goal is to produce AAA games with new technology features. You will be expected to play a fundamental role in the overall production of the team's projects.

Required Experience:	• A minimum 1+ year's mobile development experience with the *iOS* platform.
	• Strong programming knowledge and skills with using C++ or Java.
	• To have had at least a successful publication of an app/game.
	• Excellent communication and organisation skills.
	• A team player, hard worker, flexible and self-motivated.
Desirable Skills:	• Educated to degree level or equivalent, preferably in Computer Science, Engineering or Mathematics.
	• Broad knowledge and passion for the mobile games/app industry and experience with a game engine, particularly *Epic's Unreal Engine*.
	• Knowledge and experience of using *OpenGL.*

ART AND ANIMATION

What it is to be an Artist

Art and animation is the aspect of game development that brings the game to the player. Although the code from the programmers will always be running inside of the console or computer it's the artist's work that makes the game visible and concrete. Art production is the largest part of game development, either in terms of team size, its budget or the amount of data produced.

Skills and Requirements

The general production pipeline ranges from initial concepts (2D drawn or 3D clay), then to the 3D modeller (Computer based), texturing, motion-capture, animators to the final files that will be used within the game. If you want to be working in any one of these roles you will need to be able to visualise ideas and turn them into drawings or models. You will also need a strong understanding of motion, colour and the traditional arts.

Like with most **pipelines in the game industry**, no two are alike so it is a good idea to ask in your interview what the production pipeline is like within the company you are applying for.

Even if you want to only ever use the computer to create 3D models and texture you still need to learn how to draw. If you can't now, don't worry! Everyone can learn to draw and a good way to do this is to practice, if only for 10 minutes

a day drawing an object in front of you and you'll get better over time. I recommend taking life drawing lessons and also lessons on colour theory to really get ahead in the game.

Example Software/Tools

2D Software – *Adobe Photoshop* is the industry standard. It's an extremely powerful photo manipulation tool and great to learn for the creation of textures for your game assets as an artist. It can also be used in the creation of concept art along with a graphics pen tablet. A graphics tablet is used for drawing but also for 3D sculpting software such as *Pixologic's Zbrush*. It is useful as it provides the artist with the traditional pencil and paper feel for their work which is often quicker and more natural. Animators will find *Adobe Flash* a great piece of software for creating 2D animation. It'll allow you to learn the core of animation and provides you with a full professional toolset.

3D Software – For the majority of artists and animators in the game industry, extensive knowledge of the game industry is essential. It can be very daunting at first to learn but there is a vast array of tutorials out there to learn from. There are free educational versions of *Autodesk's Maya* and *3D Studio Max* both of which are widely used in not only the game but also film industry. As mentioned earlier, 3D digital sculpting tools such as *Pixologic's Zbrush* are used to digitally sculpt out a highly detailed asset. Traditional clay artists may enjoy this software and find it natural to use.

If you have never experienced any of the above software then don't panic. Anyone can learn how to use them and get the most out of them. Practice and creativity is all that's required.

Example Job Advert

Job Profile	*Junior 3D Artist*
Average Salary:	£18,000
Description:	To fulfil this job role the required candidate needs to be a talented junior/graduate assets and/or environment artist. They will have experience in creating assets for game worlds in a next gen game engine. It is essential that they understand the workflow for creating a next-gen asset using high to low poly techniques.
	This is a once in a life time opportunity to work for a globally recognised developer in the games industry creating games that will be played by thousands.
Required Experience:	A Portfolio evident with strong examples of:

- Low and High-resolution modelling in a 3D package (*Autodesk's 3Ds Max* preferred)

- High quality texture creation

- Detailed normal mapped game assets

- *Adobe Photoshop* at an industry standard level

Desirable Skills:
- Be a keen gamer
- Experience in *Crytek's CryEngine*
- Have good attention to detail
- Be able to work as part of a team.
- Have strong communication skills.

AUDIO AND SOUND

What it is to be an Audio Artist/Engineer

As an audio artist or audio engineer your job involves recording, mixing, manipulating and editing hundreds of sounds to produce a high level of immersion for the game player. If you try playing a game with the sound turned off you will swiftly realise just how important of a role it has. Sound tells the gamer how and even what they are playing, whereas the visuals tell them what is happening.

Skills and Requirements

You will need a good perception of sound as it is necessary to be able to hear sounds and mix them up enhancing the sound quality. You must make sure that what you create with sound replicates or matches that of what the game player is seeing on screen. Sometimes you will not be presented with a visual representation of a scene and will have to imagine what sound may be required for the brief of a scene you are given to work on. To become a sound engineer game companies will often require that you have a HND (or above) in Sound Engineering, or relevant in-house game audio experience.

Example Software/Tools

Waveform editors – These are editors that will allow you to manipulate and edit recorded sounds. In basic terms they work similarly to creating a text document in which you copy, paste and add effects to your text document. You can do the same for sound in a waveform editor. They are widely available and many are free so getting experience with using them shouldn't be a problem.

MIDI Sequencers – A MIDI sequencer is a software tool

that converts your chosen musical notes into sound on the instruments you want them played on. They are great tools for creating game soundtracks. Many big budget games use a full orchestral musical score.

It's also great to be able to offer your employer experience of DSP (Digital Signal Processing), Synthesizer and Effects programming.

Example Job Advert

Job Profile	*Junior Audio Designer*
Average Salary:	£18,000
Description:	The ideal candidate will have acquired their experience through a university degree or a strong personal study. The Junior Audio Designer must have knowledge on general audio recording, microphone techniques, audio editing, foley techniques/recording, field recording, dialogue recording and editing.

They will be responsible for:

- Sound editing

- Voice editing

- Music editing

- Sound creation

The Junior Audio Designer will report to the Audio Lead.

Required Experience:	•	*Soundforge* or *Wavelab* software
	•	Ability to track lay and mix audio to linear footage to commercial standards.
	•	Ability to learn new in-house audio tools and software for integrating content.
Desirable Skills:	•	Experience of *Audiokinetic's Wwise* integration.
	•	*Unity* game engine experience.
	•	Professional location and studio based sound effects recording experience.
	•	Experience recording, editing and mixing dialogue.

QUALITY ASSURANCE (QA) TESTER

What it is to be a QA Tester

A QA Tester, also known as a Games Tester, is a great way to start out in the industry. It's a great method to finding out about the various departments and general business of a games studio. As a QA Tester it is your job to seek out any mistakes and bugs that need to be fixed and communicate with the relevant team (I.e. a sound glitch to the audio department). You will have to play the game many times and although this sounds like fun for a keen gamer it gets very repetitive and in general people don't like to find out something they've made isn't working, so good people and communication skills very much helps!

Skills and Requirements

To become a games tester you are generally not required to have obtained any formal qualifications. This is because your playing skills, knowledge of games themselves and the market is the most important aspect.

You will have to be able to work under pressure and meet tight deadlines. It is also essential to have good persistence, patience, and good computer office skills.

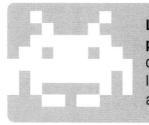

Learning some basic programming and using databases and even a foreign language will give you an advantage over other candidates!

Example Software/Tools

Reports – You will be creating a lot of reports. Make sure you are familiar with typing out clear and precise reports quickly. Becoming competent in *Microsoft's Office* is a good place to start, including the use of databases.

Some studios will use specific bug hunting software which you will be required to learn on the job.

Example Job Advert

Job Profile	*Junior QA Tester*
Average Salary:	£14,000
Description:	By joining our studio you will be stepping your foot in the door of a fantastic company full of flare and creativity. You'll gain fantastic experience working on world class AAA games.

As a QA Tester you will be required to:

- Carry out work as instructed by the QA Manager and/or QA Senior Testers
- Test games for usability, functionality, design, and compatibility flaws
- Verify and recreate bugs as required
- Identify, troubleshoot, and descriptively file bugs
- Communicate clearly with the QA Manager and the rest of the development staff

Required Experience:	• Have experience in QA games testing
	• Exceptional attention to detail and an eye for quality
	• Excellent communication skills
Desirable Skills:	• Experience with Bug Tracking software
	• At least a year of games testing experience

WRITER

What it is to be a Writer

It's an exciting time to become a Writer within the game industry. Modern games are focusing more and more on producing a 'Hollywood' style storyline and have complex and exciting plots. Gamers expect their character to have a lot of depth and be in a game world were dialogue is immersive and believable. However, many writers are still often hired on short contracts and freelance. There are many different Writer roles; audio scripts, text that appears in the game, marketing, public relations, concepts and the **Games Design Document**. The game design document contains the games backstory, character backgrounds, the plot etc. Therefore it is a technical document with a creative side.

Skills and Requirements

As you will be writing structured and naturally flowing documents you have to have an expert understanding of the language you are writing in. You must be able to spell, punctuate and produce coherent sentences to a near perfect level. As a game writer you will be working in at least one of these two categories: Fictional writing and Technical writing. You will need to be able to write creatively to create the sense of context for the player within the games plot and have general fiction writer skills as games are fiction. For the technical side you may be creating design documents or game manuals where you will be required to use your skills of organisation, conciseness and clarity to good use.

Example Software/Tools

A word processor – This is nearly everything a writer needs. It is recommended to have a full office suite, such a Microsoft's Office to be able to open and modify spread sheets and

slideshows etc. Aside from this, build up a good reference library of books and inspiration for writers like yourself. Obviously a good place to start is to have a quality dictionary and thesaurus, but there are a vast selection of books on fiction writing and storytelling.

Example Job Advert

Job Profile	*Junior Writer*

Average Salary:	£18,000

Description:	We are an award-winning independent developer founded by games industry veterans. If you're looking for a fast moving, creative environment where the work you do will make a difference, this is the place to work!
	We are seeking a talented and passionate game writer. You will have the responsibility for helping to drive the creation of our games stories. The ideal candidate will have had experience in multimedia story telling with excellent competency in game writing and a passion for games and film.
	You will be collaborating across the studio to help bring the game's story to life.
	As a Writer you will be required to:
	• Be able to evangelise the game story and narrative vision to the team.

- Work with game designers to create an effective narrative that fits with a good game design

- Revise and edit your own scripts and those of other writers

- Under the supervision of the Narrative Director, your tasks will involve enhancing the story, writing scripts and refining the pace of the game through storytelling and dialogue.

Please provide a writing example with your application.

Required Experience:
- Understanding of voice directing and editing techniques.

- Excellent communication, writing and interpersonal skills.

- Ability to work well under pressure and with deadlines.

- Passion for strong, character-driven game story content.

Desirable Skills:
- Bachelor's degree preferred, or equivalent game writing experience.

- Experience with using game engines and scripts.

The starting salary for a game developer is between £18,000 – £25,000. However, your income will vary greatly depending on your experience and the nature of the studio you are working for. Starting out as a QA tester may see a dramatic loss in starting salary but is a very valid and viable way to enter the game industry with little experience.

Show proof of your enthusiasm. When applying for a job within the game industry employers will want to see proof of not only your knowledge but also your passion for games and the industry. One way to do this is to attend game events, expos and stay up-to-date with industry news through game related magazines and websites.

CHAPTER FOUR
THE IMPORTANCE OF NETWORKING

WHAT IS NETWORKING?

Networking is a superb way of building contacts and finding opportunities for your career as a game designer. By connecting, building relationships, constructing value for others and earning the trust of other professionals is central in taking you to the peak of your career. You can network at any stage of your career and it's nearly all completely free.

It's not whom you know but rather it's who knows you.

Traditionally networking is done face to face, normally at an arranged event where you go up to someone and have a chat about each other's backgrounds and what they hope to achieve in the future. While this is still probably the best method the internet has brought new ways to network and they also must be fully utilised.

WHY YOU SHOULD BE NETWORKING

In your free time it is essential to network – Your skills, talents and even experience will never get you anywhere if nobody knows you exist. It can be great for young industry starters who can gain a lot of experience from industry professionals through networking. Networking can also often help motivate you and push you to take your work to the next level and expand your industry knowledge.

Here are some reasons why you should network:

- It builds confidence
- It helps you discover jobs not yet published to the public
- It engages your connections to help with your search
- It expands your network connections

Many people who have shy personalities will find that when networking they become much more open and talkative as they are talking about a subject that they enjoy and know a lot about. You will be surrounded by like-minded individuals so don't be put off if you are shy! Another misconception about networking is that it takes too much time and effort. You will have to put a lot of time and effort into networking but the rewards far outweigh those of the effort you have to put in.

By putting in a lot of time and effort into networking the rewards you can get could be huge. Networking can in fact save you time and effort in the long run because once you have your connections, things that you may want; help, advice or a job, may only be a telephone call away for you. This would save a lot of time and frustration and at a relatively low cost. Building a network is an investment, if you stick with it, it will grow.

HOW AND WHERE TO NETWORK

There are many ways to network but the best way to start networking is with existing contacts. Anyone you know, even related or not to the game industry – friends, teachers, classmates from school, developers, recruiters – anybody. You don't have to arrange meetings or a gathering to network, you can give them a call or drop them an email. It is very important to make sure that your initial goal is to help them and understand their needs before you tell them your own. Networking is a two way street. You should only be asking them for favours once you have given some value to them. You will find that by showing an interest, being polite and providing value to others will give you a far more stronger and reliable network, one willing to help you in your pursuit for industry success.

Do not dismiss anyone as irrelevant. You may want to become a game programmer but that doesn't mean anyone outside of the programming or even the game sector should not be worth your time to network with. One day that online blogger may help spread the word about a game you created or worked on. Make sure you network beyond the game industry.

Attending game events, expos and showcases are great opportunities. Places such as the London Expo, *Eurogamer Expo* are great places to meet industry professionals and like minded people. When attending such events, always carry

a business card that you can give to anyone you networked with. Network specific events, such as those found on www.videogame.meetups.com is a great place to find networking events to attend.

 **Stay connected** after you make new contacts. Make sure you follow up with anyone you have networked with. This includes who accepts you as a friend or a connection on social media such as LinkedIn or Twitter, people from events or current/previous colleagues.

Networking online is one of the most powerful tools available to your pursuit in becoming a game designer. Social media is the place to network and is the least time and money consuming yet extremely rewarding outlet. Connecting with people via LinkedIn is one of the best networking methods you can do. It is probably the number one place that industry recruiters go to search for new talent and it contains nearly every person within the game industry in one place.

When using LinkedIn you can:

- Join groups and discussions full of industry professionals who, if you are providing active input, will take notice of you.
- Connect with everyone you know
- Connect with everyone related to your job specialisation! Add game industry recruiters, people from game studios and generally as many people as you can. You will find that when you add someone they

will check your profile out to see who you are.

- Make your profile professional and advertise yourself on it clearly outlining what work you are looking for and make it very clear you are currently seeking work.

LinkedIn – Make your surname "Looking for work!"

On your LinkedIn profile change your surname to something that demonstrates you are looking for work this means that when you add someone or if a recruiter is looking through their connections they will know straight away that you are worth their time talking to.

Search for people, jobs, companies, and more...

Home   Profile   Network   Jobs   Interests

Save $100 Limited Time - DreamHost Web Hosting, Limitless storage, bandwidth, doma

Joshua Brown - Looking for Work!
3D Artist

United Kingdom | Computer Games

Current	Sim720, Enraged Entertainment
Previous	Tripmine Studios, What Comics Entertainment, RBC Investor Services
Education	University of Derby

Improve your profile   Edit ▼

185
connections

uk.linkedin.com/pub/joshua-brown-looking-for-work/64/263/464   Contact Info

Make sure you have active profiles on other social media too, such as Facebook and Twitter. Forums are a great place to meet people similar to you and also established industry professionals, again making it a successful way to network

with like-minded people in an online community. Use these people to your advantage by learning from each other, ask questions, post work for feedback etc. Online forums such as www.polycount.com are well worth checking out. Remember, help others on these forums as by doing so you will be remembered and they will be much more likely to help you out in the future.

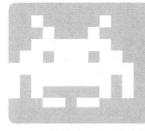

Make your favourite online forum your home page to stay current, the games industry is a fast moving one and ever changing so staying up to date is essential.

Sometimes the best networking opportunities can come from real work. By volunteering yourself for helping out for free on online projects (which are widely available) you gain valuable knowledge, contacts and experience to put on your CV. In the current App store craze we are in, everyone has the opportunity to create games and publish them, be one of these people and get noticed.

Emails are easy to send but just as easy to ignore. Sending out emails is often a quick way to network it isn't always the most efficient. If you can get hold of your contacts phone number then giving them a call is much more personal and shows you care. Plus they cannot ignore you this way!

Ultimately, networking is well worth your investment of time and effort. Sharing useful information and connecting like-minded people are simple actions that everyone will appreciate. You will open up a lot more opportunities by networking.

CHAPTER FIVE
EDUCATION

This chapter of the book is dedicated to the preparation you can make via your education. There are many stages to education and you may not currently be in an educational position. Therefore this chapter will describe many various different stages and offer advice no matter what stage of education you may be in.

SCHOOL

To start, if you are still young and at school then it is too soon for you to devote all your attention to becoming a game designer as you are not yet ready for this degree of specialisation. This is your time to experiment and try different areas you may find interesting, you may well find out that you have a passion for a different industry as time goes on. However, use this time to find out what you are good at and what you enjoy doing. If you enjoy creativity and arts you may desire to become a game artist. In this case

keep on practising and experiment with the different possible avenues (drawing, digital art, animation etc.). Do you enjoy writing school plays or stories? Is music your favourite class? Have you tried composing your own music? Ask yourself these types of questions and if you don't know the answers, try them out. This way you will be able to uncover your talent.

Nearly every subject at school can be applied to computer game development. For example science; scientific elements are implemented in most games: gravity, optics, aerodynamics, physics and anatomy is very useful to artists. Many games are set within different historical time periods and having an understanding of what it was like living in a particular time will only benefit the believability of the game world you help create. Many jobs in the game industry require math, especially the programming ones where you'll find Algebra, geometry and trigonometry are required. The list goes on, so make the most of your time at school and give everything a try!

By the time you reach your A-levels you will probably have a rough idea what path you'd like to take – don't worry if you do not, just focus on what you enjoy. Tailor your subject accordingly so that if for example you want to become a writer you may choose to study English, Media studies and ICT.

There are many ways to set out your career path and higher education is not the only way to achieving a job within the game industry. As long as you have the determination, passion and you produce good work then a development studio will take notice.

UNIVERSITY

If you feel university is something that you will enjoy or benefit from then it is definitely something you should do. Not only will competing with someone who has a degree be more difficult if you yourself do not have one, by going to university it will provide you with the depth and experience needed to becoming a professional game designer. There are many universities in the United Kingdom that offer game specific and game related courses (see **Appendix A**, for a thorough list of the available courses and Universities).

If you decide to go to university finding a course best suited to you may be hard to find. However, within the UK there are many game related courses out there of a high standard. *The University of Derby's Computer Game Modelling and Animation* course is excellent for example. If you want to become an artist of some sort then a course like this, which doesn't constrain you to only tradition, 2D or 3D art or even animation may be ideal for you as it allows you to find your desired career path.

It is often said that if you want to become a programmer you should chose a computer science degree instead of a game specific one. This is not necessarily true. Modern courses offer great options for transferable skills.

When choosing a university, look out for courses that offer a work placement year. These courses are the best ones to choose as you are far more likely to get a job within the industry if you have some kind of experience. Aside from that it is often the best way to learn.

If you're a thinking of heading to university make sure you visit in person the universities you want to apply to and find out everything you can about the course, especially these questions:

Is the course producing a first class show reel of its students? Are the students getting jobs after university? What facilities does it offer? And what is its dropout rate like?

If you feel you have made a mistake in your course choice, most courses will allow you to make a switch so bare that in mind.

KNOWING WHAT TO STUDY

Knowing what to study can be difficult if you are still unsure on what career path you want to take but by now you should be familiar with your own skills, abilities and what you enjoy. Use these factors to make a decision on the area of study you will take at university level. Many courses out there will be focused on Art, Programming, Audio Development etc. and will allow for flexibility within those areas. For example the Computer Game Modelling and Animation course at the *University of Derby* (again, see **Appendix A**, for the full list of available courses and Universities) will allow you pursue a career as an Animator, a Concept Artist, Environment Artist, Prop Artist and so on.

A few years back it was considered the best advice for study was to specialise and get as much experience in that speciality as you can. For example become a great artificial intelligence programmer or 3D character modeller so that you will be able to convince a developer that your skills are the ones missing from their current team. However, although that still stands to some degree it's also becoming increasingly more common for developers to want well rounded employees, for instance those who are fantastic programmers yet who can also design and have good artistic skills. Make sure that you are always open minded and willing to learn new things. In a creative industry like the

game industry you will be constantly learning new software, processes and skills.

Be vigilant of any course that advertises itself to be 'intensive'. A course that is only two years opposed to one may not be a good thing. It isn't about how quickly a course or a tutor can throw knowledge at you, it is the quality of the course. Make sure you choose a course that is at the right pace for you. It is not possible to become a master audio artist in a few months.

TOP TEN WAYS TO GET THE MOST OUT OF YOUR TIME STUDYING

1. Stay positive. The bulk of scholars taking a game specific degree will become a professional game designer. The degree is your passage to a fascinating career.

2. Are you making yourself known? Build and maintain an active online presence. A great way of doing this is creating a blog and updating your portfolio week by week. This all adds to your CV.

3. Don't let social media be your downfall. Your online profile includes any website that you post on. All your hard effort of getting noticed as an up and coming

game designer could be ruined by a stray comment on *Facebook*.

4. Work on skills that your game design course doesn't specifically teach. Creative writing, public speaking, programming (if you're not on a programming course) for example will really help you stand out when you go looking for a job.

5. Practice, practice and practice. The more practice you get, the closer you will be to becoming a game designer. Your expertise needs to be as natural to you as eating a meal.

6. Take part in Game events. These can be events where gamers get together and play games or events where someone talks about games. Get involved. There is also a great 'game camp' event called the *x48* which is sponsored by *Microsoft*. The x48 is a game creation marathon over forty-eight hours in which many universities across the United Kingdom take part in.

7. Be brave and bold, publish your work for others. App stores on mobile devices are great for this and can really push you to develop your skills and learn from feedback.

8. If your course offers industry experience, take it. Any experience you can get is vital and will give you a huge boost over students graduating without any. Plus it is said on average to boost your final year grades by an entire classification.

9. Keep organised. To some it may come naturally but if not it is certainly something anyone can learn. Plan when all work has to be in and set yourself targets and goals to achieve things by certain times.

10. Have fun! It is important to not only enjoy your work but enjoy your time outside of studies. Be sure to socialise

and get involved with university activities. This will not only allow for vital destress time but the people you meet could potentially be a great person to network with in the future or even be your partner.

WITHOUT FURTHER EDUCATION

If you are not in education and do not fancy it, do not worry. A game design job is still very much achievable through the points mentioned in this book and especially through the development of your portfolio. You can learn nearly all software without a degree, and in fact it is essential that you learn and develop your specialised skills and software at home as often as you can, whether you are in a degree or not. Show off your latest developed skills in your portfolio. If you do not go on to further education then make sure you are dedicated to learning and practising at home and take part in online communities, sharing your work for critique and asking for advice. You will find many experienced industry professionals online willing to give their help.

If you are not in further education a great way to develop and get industry experience is to **join an independent studio or online community team**. You can find literally hundreds of teams online looking for volunteers to help on projects and make games. These games are often remakes of old games being made by their fans.

JOINING THE GAME INDUSTRY FROM PREVIOUSLY UNRELATED JOBS

If you plan on becoming a game designer from an industry unrelated, the door is very much wide open. As well as following the advice previously written in this book there are other ways you can prepare. Firstly, make sure that you play games and have a passion for them. This will be a common requirement for nearly every job role as a developer. Secondly, play games and analyse them. Look at how they are structured and put together. Take notes and write down your thoughts, what did you like? And what did you not? Make sure to play many different genres and study a variety of games. By doing these things you set yourself up to entering the game industry as QA tester, getting your foot in the door. Like all job application processes, be persistent. Call everyday asking for an interview or to chase up on your CV. Hard work and determination will pay off.

CHAPTER SIX
CV – CURRICULUM VITAE (RESUME)

When applying for a job in the game industry your application should include three things:

- A cover letter
- A CV/Resume
- A Portfolio

It's not a better or more talented person who will get a job, it is the most prepared.

WHAT IS A CV?

Your CV is a very important document that should demonstrate you have the required skills, potential and experience to fulfil the job role you are applying for. An effective CV will match the specifications of those that the employer has listed in the jobs advert and description.

A new CV for every job. Never send the same CV to every job you apply for. Your CV should be tailored for each job application even for the same job role for EVERY job you apply for. Each employer will list their own desired requirements that they want an applicant to offer. Read the job description and then reread it. Then tailor your CV to match it.

The job description is the blueprint

The job description is the blueprint for the role you are applying for and for your CV to match that job. When you look at a job advert it is important to look out for the key words they use to describe a candidate's skills and requirements. If a job advert requires the ideal candidate to "be flexible and self-motivated" then make sure you put that you are flexible and self-motivated clearly in your own CV before you apply!

Many applicants can be tempted to lie on their CV and state they have expert knowledge in software, qualifications and skills that they do not have. **Always be honest.** It's not worth lying as you will eventually get caught out and employers can still dismiss you for it months or even years later.

HOW TO MAKE YOU OWN CV

Let us take a look at an example CV, this one being for a 3D artist:

Note: This CV is not in the typical order of traditional structure as it is designed for someone who has little long-term game industry experience. However, a more traditional structure will be covered after.

Joshua **Brown**   *3D Artist*

🏠 My Portfolio:
www.JoshuaBrown3D.com

✉ 07000 0212000
exampleemail@example.com

Profile

Ever since I played my first video game I knew that I wanted to be the one making them. Since that day I set my academic and career path to achieving this goal and continue to do so with great drive and passion. I thrive in team environments where ideas are shared and new skills are learnt.

Skills & Attributes

- BA (Hons) Degree
- Realistic Environments
- Texturing
- Modular Assets

- Thrive in Team Environments
- High to Low Polygon Workflow
- Advanced Material Shaders
- Foliage and Organic Assets

Software

Competent and extensive knowledge in:

Intermediate skill in:

- Maya & 3D Studio Max 2014
- Photoshop CS5
- Unity 3.5
- GameMaker: Studio

- Unreal Development Kit 4
- Crazybump
- CryEngine 3
- nDo2 & dDo 2.0

- ZBrush 4.0
- Microsoft Office
- Headus UV Layout
- Adobe Flash CS5

Education and Qualifications

University of Example
2006-2009

BA (Hons) Computer Games Animation and Modelling

Secondary School
1999-2006

A Levels: Product Design, Information Technology, Media Studies and Film Studies
GCSE: 11 A*- C grade passes

Employment

2014 – Present

Example Game Studio, Modification team
3D Artist (www.examplegamestudio.com)
- Creating 3D Game Assets
- Working to team Feedback
- Expressed the artistic goals and direction of the mod
- Created Highly detailed textures for a FPS viewpoint

2012 – 2014

Example Work Experience, London Game Development Studio
3D Environment Artist
- Completed work to tight deadlines for the London 2012 Olympics producing highly detailed 3D assets.

Notice that this CV clearly defines the role in which it is seeking, a 3D art job. The 'Profile' is specific and relevant to games industry and the job role (3D Artist) in which the CV is tailored for. Although there is an 'Education' section, it mentions right at the top of the page the highest qualification. A University degree gets noticed. The 'Skills & Attributes' section is used to demonstrate the key skills that match the job description. If you are applying for animation, programming, art, QA and most jobs in a game development studio you will need to create a 'software' section on your CV to list the software you know and what version. There are lots of white space and the text is consistent and clear to read, something like 'Arial point-12' is good. Small touches such as the icons next to the contact information make the CV more interesting than the standard page of text and show off some creativity. It's worth noting **the most relevant Game work experience is on the first page.**

If you lack experience, maybe you're just out of education or making a career change, you can list voluntary work or short term work in your 'Employment/Experience' section but instead of giving exact dates provide the start year and finish year.

HOW TO STRUCTURE YOUR OWN CV

It may vary from role to role but a general outline and structure you can follow for a Game Specific CV is to:

- Begin with your **contact details** (your name, your online portfolio, phone number and e-mail address).

- Your **profile** (what your goal and job role is that you're after, relevant personal information such as "Writing the storylines for games is something I have always had great desire for" and include keywords which best describe your character).

- **Employment/Experience** – Complete this section in reverse chronological order. Include employment dates, locations, job titles, and brief descriptions of the responsibilities you achieved.

- **Skills/Attributes** – Use positive keywords to describe yourself. For example: "Passionate", "Self-motivated", "Strong leadership skills", "Attention to detail", "Positive attitude".

- **Software** – For most roles within the games industry you will be required to know various programs and software. Many studios have their own proprietary software. List the software you have knowledge in and the version.

- **Education** – List your most recent qualifications first, including degrees, additional training and anything that you've been awarded that's relevant to your job

- **Personal Interests** – Be clever as to what you put here. Just like the rest of your CV make it relevant to the game job you are applying for. Photography is a great

one for artists, writers can list books that inspire them or blogs they write etc.

Do not pad your CV out. It is a very common misconception that having more words in a CV is best. It's not, in fact lots of white space is a good thing, making it clearer and easier to read. It's about quality over quantity. Make sure you **create a positive image of yourself.** Is it neat and clear? Are there any grammar, punctuation or spelling mistakes?

A CREATIVE OR CONVENTIONAL CV, WHICH IS BEST?

You are in a creative industry so why not make a creative CV to show off your own creativity? Many people find when switching to a creative CV after months of using a conventional CV with no luck, they start to get picked up on companies and agencies radars. However, it is very important to stress that without fully understanding what it takes to make a great conventional CV you may as well not bother creating a creative version. Therefore a creative CV should be created after you've made a conventional one and be used very conscientiously as conventional CVs are much more widely accepted. A creative CV looks good when advertising yourself on your website/online portfolio while using your conventional CV to go out and apply for jobs may be an effective method.

Here are some examples of creative CVs:

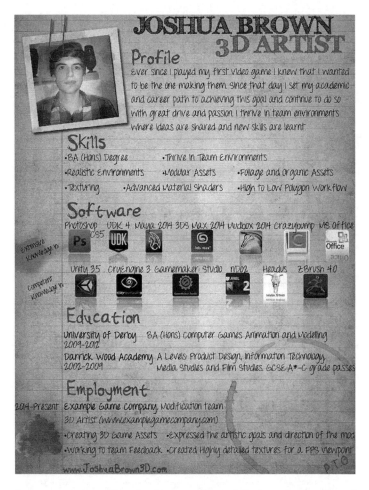

JOSHUA BROWN
3D ARTIST

Profile

Ever since I played my first video game I knew that I wanted to be the one making them. Since that day I set my academic and career path to achieving this goal and continue to do so with great drive and passion. I thrive in team environments where ideas are shared and new skills are learnt.

Skills

- BA (Hons) Degree
- Thrive in Team Environments
- Realistic Environments
- Modular Assets
- Foliage and Organic Assets
- Texturing
- Advanced Material Shaders
- High to Low Polygon Workflow

Software

Extensive knowledge in:
Photoshop CS5, UDK 4, Maya 2014, 3DS Max 2014, Mudbox 2014, Crazybump, MS Office

Competent knowledge in:
Unity 3.5, Cryengine 3, Gamemaker: Studio, nDo2, Headus, ZBrush 4.0

Education

University of Derby   BA (Hons) Computer Games Animation and Modelling
2009-2012

Darrick Wood Academy A Levels: Product Design, Information Technology,
2002-2009   Media Studies and Film Studies. GCSE A*-C grade passes

Employment

2014-Present Example Game Company, Modification team
3D Artist (www.examplegamecompany.com)
- Creating 3D Game Assets
- Expressed the artistic goals and direction of the mod
- Working to team Feedback
- Created Highly detailed textures for a FPS viewpoint

www.JoshuaBrown3D.com

As you can see, they look very different from a conventional CV and this is partially the point, they stand out and hopefully if they are good enough will draw the attention of the employer. Employers can get hundreds of CVs for any particular job, do what you can to get noticed and remembered for the right reasons.

If you have an email address that looks similar to this 'xpantha-girlx@example.com' do not use it. You need a **professional email address.** A great tip for this is to use your websites URL as the '@example.com'. It looks very professional and well thought out if employers are contacting you at 'JoB-loggs@JoBloggs2DArtist.com' as opposed to the standard email formats.

WRITING A COVER LETTER

Every CV that you send off should be accompanied by a cover letter. Your cover letter is your first chance to make a good impression so a lot of care should be put into it. For example, your cover letter should be specific to the position you are applying for and it should relate to your skills and experience to those posted in the job's advert. It should include knowledge of the role and why you are suited to fill that role.

Here are a few tips to follow when creating your cover letter:

- Make your letter unique by avoiding statements made all the time such as 'I have excellent interpersonal skills'.

- Show that you know and care about the employer by mentioning them and tailoring yourself to the company.

- Do not use abbreviations.

- Less is more. Never exceed more than a page, 3-4 paragraphs is the sweet spot.

- Your cover letter may be skim-read so include game industry keywords.

- Subtly flatter the company by recognising them for an achievement. For instance '*Example Company* is known for being at industry forefront in artificial intelligence'

- You must have someone you trust check and then re-check your letter. There is no room for spelling, grammar and punctuation errors!

- Follow up your letter and CV with a phone call, e-mail or office visit.

Dear Mr Thompson,

I have the knowledge, experience, and determination to be the next 3D artist for *Example Company*. There are many things I can contribute to the art department.

My time spent volunteering with *Example Experience* honed my skills as a *3D artist* by working to tight deadlines, with ambitious people and achieving published work praised by my colleagues for my attention to form, detail and style on my game assets.

At the beginning of my career I graduated from the University of *Example* with a *BA (Hons) in Game*

Design. At the beginning of my career I graduated from the University of Example with a BA (Hons) in Game Design. This degree allowed my creativity as an artist to grow and it was here that I became a mentor, further developing my skills. I have since led groups of artists in constructive critiques and fostered an environment of collabora-tive thinking.

Peer review is an integral part of my work. It's allowed me to grow as an individual with expert skills as a 3D modeller and texturer and keeps me producing new and fresh work using current and next-gen techniques. I am an active member of online forums and enjoy receiving and providing feedback in those communities. As a professional artist and mentor my drive is to succeed in delivering results.

If hired, I will approach all tasks with enthusiasm and drive. I am truly passionate about the games industry and I look forward to furthering the artistic evolution of *Example Company's* games. My portfolio can be found at http://www.JoshuaBrown3D.com and I enclose my CV for your information.

Thank you for your time and consideration.

Sincerely,

Joshua Brown
3D Environment Artist
www.JoshuaBrown3D.com

You can find many templates and further information regarding CVs online at www.CVwritingSkills.co.uk

CHAPTER SEVEN

BUILD A PORTFOLIO THAT GETS YOU YOUR JOB

THE IMPORTANCE OF GOOD REFERENCES

In this case not written job references, but rather references of material in your chosen expertise. For example if you are a 3D artist whatever you're working on finding good references and lots of it is essential. If you are an artist for example and your task is to model a table, gather reference photographs of the exact or very similar table that you are going to model in 3D and look at how it is built in reality and this affects the way you go about modelling and designing your own.

Gather references for inspiration – writer books, art images etc. When building your portfolio or working on a project in the industry gathering good references is essential.

There is a vast amount of information on portfolios out there, online and in books. Spending the time perfecting your

portfolio cannot be overstated. You have to keep it current and show only your best work. Your portfolio will land you your interview so make sure it is up to industry standard. Best way to see if it is, play games, look at other peoples portfolios but never ever copy.

Produce an online portfolio, a .zip portfolio for email, a printed copy and also a disc version for post. Remember it is key to only include your best work – do not pad it out with everything you've ever done. If you look at some of your work and think "I could do that better" do it. Put your favourite work at the front as recruiters will often only scan the first few pages. There are many more tips I could provide for creating a professional and stand out portfolio but the best thing for you to do is make it and perfect it from feedback by others, such as friends, family and most importantly industry professionals on online forums and internet discussions.

The only job you won't really need a portfolio for is a QA tester.

So, where to begin? When making your portfolio, whether it contains images, text, video, models or sounds; they have to be your own. It should show off the skills and creations to make reviewers impressed with you, not your ability to reference other people's work. Any hint of plagiarism will result in your application being discarded and you being put on a 'blacklist'.

These days it is essential to have an online portfolio as well as a hard copy one. Starting with the hard copy, let us assume you are a concept artist. When you turn up to your interview you will be presenting your portfolio and its presentation is very important.

Make sure your concept drawings are displayed in a high quality folder and you have a consistent presentation theme.

For example:

London Post-Apocalyptic Concept Art - Joshua Brown   www.JoshuaBrown3D.com

Autumn Stream - Joshua Brown   www.JoshuaBrown3D.com

As you can see, both images have the same bar at the bottom with the same styles and format. Generally each image should have your name and some details on it somewhere, but this is more relevant for the online aspect as when you post them in forums or anywhere online it is an advertisement of yourself and your ability.

Some basic skills in imaging software such as *Adobe's Photoshop* should be enough to be able to present your work nicely as images. This applies mostly to the artists but regardless of your job role you should always format and display your work in a consistent and professional manner.

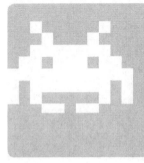

All work you make for your portfolio you should post in online forums to **get feedback**. You will receive criticism but this is part of the process of learning and perfecting your skills to produce the best possible work.

As a game designer you must have a website. These are cheap and easy to obtain so it should be a simple process. Make your domain name relevant to you and your work, i.e. www.JoshuaBrown3D.comorwww.ExampleNameAudio.com. You can obtain a domain name online for less than £5. When it comes to building your website, there are many free ways to do this. Wordpress.com, blogspot.com are all great ways. You don't need to create a super fancy and creative website so long as your work shows off your ability and creativity. It is far more important for your website to be simple to use and for your best work to be presented as soon as it's loaded up.

Here are a few examples:

Example one

Example two

These are some top tips to ensure a persuading portfolio:

- Show off your skills – Create a variety of assets using as many different programs and tools as possible. It's extremely desirable to show off – so go all out! Try to hook the reviewer by revealing your most eye-catching work first, and then ensure you have plenty of other assets in there. Make deliberate, signposted details of the tools you have used to make them. Adding in at least a few examples of detailed creation stills is a good idea.

- It is extremely important to avoid plagiarism; if a reviewer recognises even a minor part of your portfolio as being from another book or tutorial, then it is very likely that your application will be discarded.

- You will be judged in particular as an artist almost entirely by your portfolio – so make it count! Ensure that it is original and stand-out in order to impress recruiters. Create ground-up themes, assets and information to make a stunning portfolio.

- Make sure it is well rounded. Whilst your most impressive work should be what catches the reviewers eye first, you also want to prove that you are competent, flexible and experienced. Show that you can handle the basics as well as more complex work, prove by creation stills that you know your stuff and get a good balance of written and visual information.

- A portfolio is with you for the long haul. You should constantly add to it with new things you've learned or be tweaking and testing different themes and layouts.

- For Artists – Adding your own reference photos or concept art (or both) to things you have then gone on to make is very impressive as it again proves you

have a set of well-rounded skills. These photos could include real world environments or the photo used for a nice texture. Taking stills of an extremely high quality rendering and comparing it side by side to a reference photo/concept art, even if it could never actually run as a game, is striking.

- For Programmers – Make a game demo that is playable, show your own custom algorithms and custom tools. You should demonstrate that you have the ability to code in C/C++ and also C# if you wish to develop tools. Your portfolio doesn't need to look extremely fancy just layout your work in a clear, presentable manner showing the scripts you've made and the end result.

- For Writers – consider adding these types of writing to your portfolio:

  ◊ A creative piece that shows you have the ability to paint vivid pictures with words

  ◊ A piece from the web on a specific topic.

  ◊ A report you have created for your studies or community project

  ◊ An essay or other writing project that demonstrates your ability to analyse and solve a problem and/or argue a point of view.

  ◊ An example of a collaboratively written document, accompanied with this you should also include a description on how the team worked together and details of your contribution.

  ◊ A multimedia presentation

  ◊ A Blog

- Concept art goes especially well with something completely new – a fantasy world, something futuristic or your own posing hero. Concept art should usually be of a high quality and be stylised (preferably to something that complements the arts subject matter).

Your portfolio is your opportunity to show off everything you can do. It should be eye-catching, balanced and well filled with high quality examples of your work replete with creation stills and reference photos. And remember to not be shy about showing off!

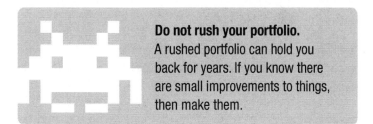

Do not rush your portfolio.
A rushed portfolio can hold you back for years. If you know there are small improvements to things, then make them.

HOW TO DECIDE WHAT TO INCLUDE

This depends on the job you want. If you want to work on creating environments in games tailor your portfolio to this and make environments, environment assets or build worlds in your scripts. If you're happy to do anything or you are still unsure what position you want to specialise in you should keep everything as generic as possible at this point in time. Try to show off your creativity as much as you can, enough people out there fill their portfolios with Sci-fi corridors or a shinny Lamborghini. Make something rustic, unique and of your own design.

WHAT NOT TO INCLUDE

Here are a few things you shouldn't include in your portfolio:

Poor standard of work – Any mistakes will stand out like a sore thumb and is not something you want to be remembered for. Even worse, if you do not notice the mistakes yourself and them being brought up in your interview. Your interviewer will wonder what other unnoticed mistakes you'll make when working for them.

Unfinished work – This is not a good sign for two reasons. It will demonstrate you don't finish tasks properly and secondly it will not demonstrate your work at its best. The only time it can be condoned is if the work is looking great/functions well and has been designed specifically for an interview you are attending. For example if you are applying to *Polyphony Digital*, the creators or *Gran Turismo*, then having a portfolio of car sound effects, car physics code or car models will help your opportunity of success by demonstrating you can do the work they require and it proves you have a passion for the work they do. If it is unfinished let them know that when showing it and tell them you created it in preparation for their interview.

Old work – Work in the game industry gets outdated fairly quickly. Keep your portfolio fresh and current by always working on it.

DON'T BE AFRAID TO ASK FOR HELP

There are a vast amount of online forums and portfolio websites to post your work to, whether it's coding, art, writing or audio. There are many game specific ones too such as www.gamedev.net and www.polycount.com. Here you will

find fellow game designers that will critique you. You will be facing some of the industry's best game designers so brace yourself for the high level of standards and competition. The comments and advice you will get from these people in the online communities is invaluable and the best part is, it is completely free.

Posting your work for others to see and comment on is probably the best advice you can get when trying to build a portfolio, whatever stage you are at. It will help you grow and develop as a game designer in any field. Sometimes people will tell you not to include a piece of work that you really like. If the majority of people think this, then it's probably best you don't include it but by all means keep it in a personal portfolio.

Create an online blog and post work frequently to demonstrate to potential employers your dedication and activeness. It's also a great way for people to notice your work, comment on it and help you improve along the way!

S.M.A.R.T.

Using the S.M.A.R.T. goals is a commonly used technique and is taught in many industries. S.M.A.R.T. stands for Specific, Measurable, Achievable, Realistic, and Timed. It a fantastic way to plan and accurately estimate the work and time it'll take for you to accomplish a task.

For example, if you have an interview for a first person shooter games company (a shooter game played from a first person

camera perspective) coming up you may use the S.M.A.R.T. technique to plan the creation of some audio sound effects for some gun assets; you may apply it like this:

Specific – Three new sound effects for two gun assets for my online portfolio.

Measurable – You will look at the standard of sound effects out there, especially those used in the company you are preparing for. List everything you will need to do: Record the sounds, edit them, apply them to the guns in a game engine.

Achievable – You will then estimate the time you think it will take to achieve each task and compare that to the time you have available to actually spend working on it each day.

Realistic – Do you have enough time each day to work on it and get it done in time for the upcoming interview? Are you taking too much on and is it worthwhile to spend all your time on this?

Timed – Set your project to be finished in time for that upcoming interview and delegate deadlines for when each piece should be finished by.

Due to the fact that a reviewer of your work may only look at the first few pages of your portfolio it is very important to put your best work at the front or in their view first. It does not matter if you are sending your work through email, disc or printed, put the best work at the front.

If you put your work on disc or in a .zip format make sure that it is labelled clearly and whoever uses it will not have to install or download anything out of the ordinary.

Some studios will get junior employees to look through applicant's portfolios and decide whether it should be considered further. This can be a good thing if your work isn't

at its best but the majority of the time, someone who has lots of experience will look at your portfolio and will spend a matter of seconds deciding whether it's worth their time looking further than the first page.

Your final piece of your portfolio should also be one of your favourites as you will want the viewer to feeling good about your work. All work should be presented in a clear folder, leather is best. Discs should be clearly labelled with your name, contact details and website. Content on the disc should be labelled with your name, i.e. 'JoshuaBrown_ Article_01.jpg'.

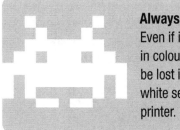

Always scan your work in colour. Even if it's a pencil drawing scan it in colour as all the grey tones will be lost if you use the black and white settings on a scanner and printer.

WHERE TO FIND JOBS AND HOW TO APPLY

You can apply directly to companies that are currently hiring through game magazines and websites of the country you work in. A great magazine for this in the United Kingdom is *Edge* magazine and also *Develop*, with *Edge* being readily available at most newsagents. Try applying directly through specific game company's websites, even if they do not have a position that is yet listed as this may provide you a head start over other potential candidates. www.gamasutra.com and www.gamesindustry.biz are great places of resource when looking for available jobs.

Another great method is through recruitment agencies. Make sure when signing up to them that you give them your best possible CV and portfolio attachments as they will consider you for many jobs but in this instance you won't be able to tailor your CV for each one individually. You can find great success through recruitment agencies for relatively little work. But they will often take a percentage of your starting salary if you are successful in getting a job through them. This can be up to thirty per cent. If you do apply through a recruitment agency call them up on a regular basis, at least weekly, for an update.

LinkedIn is another powerful resource for finding jobs. Many companies will advertise through it and many people are recruiting on it so join groups and add as many connections as you can and if you are making people aware of your situation you will soon find people offering you work.

Always ask for feedback if unsuccessful. If you are unsuccessful in your application you can always ask for feedback, especially if you failed at a test or interview. This is great information to help you improve for your next attempt elsewhere.

CHAPTER EIGHT
INTERVIEW

Competition for jobs is fierce and therefore you need to be well prepared and at your best. For many, interviews can be a nerve-wracking experience and many also believe you have to answer every question correctly or even perfectly. However, this is simply not true. You will need to understand the games industry, have good knowledge on your role and the company you're applying for but it's not all technical ability, you can easily get the job over someone who has more experience, more software skills etc. through preparation, the way you portray yourself and your likeability factor.

PROS MAKE A PLAN

Interviews are designed to assess your potential to perform a job role. In the gaming industry they are normally structured around roughly 10 questions (questions I will discuss later) and they will also tell you about the company, specifics on

your role and who you'll be working with. By understanding what your potential employer is looking for you will drastically increase your chances of success.

An interview is your chance to shine and your chance to show the interviewer that you are the right person for the role.

USING THE JOB DESCRIPTION

One of the best ways to prepare for the interview is similar to that of tailoring your CV. Get a copy of the job description and find areas that match yourself. If they say they want someone who is "Proficient in *Epic's Unreal Engine*", tell them the experience you have in this engine and prove it by telling or showing them something you've made using it. Try to use this method when answering all questions in an interview. Don't just tell the interviewer you are a 'Hard worker'; prove it to them by telling them a situation that demonstrates you are indeed a hard worker.

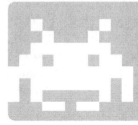

Remember to look out for **keywords in the job description;** "Passionate", "Self-motivated", "a team player". Use these words when describing yourself.

Make sure as part of your preparation you find out background the company you are applying too. You should know what games they have made, who the main staff are and also what they are currently working on. If you can't manage to find out what they are currently working on then this gives you a fantastic question to ask in your interview. It is very important to arrive to the interview with this kind of preparation as it not

only shows the interviewer that you care enough about the job to put the effort in, but it will also give you confidence.

First Impressions are lasting impressions. Within the first few seconds the interviewer will have made their mind up to whether they like you, all based on your appearance and presentation. Dress well, smile, show confidence, look at them in the eyes and shake their hands firmly and try to not sit statically throughout the interview (you can use hand gestures when talking etc.).

YOUR PORTFOLIO IS YOUR FRIEND

When you turn up to any interview you should bring samples of your best work. This should be presented well and it's often a great way to get out of situations where you're not sure what to say and how to answer something. Point to your work and start describing the thought and workflow behind it. This works especially well if you are applying for an art position as showing off a fancy game asset of environment will distract their attention away from any previous awkwardness.

Many people turn up to interviews with laptops, tablets and even their phones to show video demonstrations of their work. This can be a great thing to do but make sure it doesn't require any faffing about and that you have it easily at hand.

Make sure that it won't receive any incoming calls etc. while your interview is going on.

The game industry if often relaxed in terms of employees clothing and many people dress casually for work. However, your interviewers will often be senior staff and be well dressed. **Turn up well tailored in smart clothes,** this contributes to that all important first impression and you can always dress down once you have the job.

STAY POSITIVE

Interviews may not always feel like they are going to plan but you can never be sure so stay positive and keep up you enthusiasm. You don't need to know the answer to every question and if you haven't answered a question well use your portfolio to distract and focus on your achievements.

Make sure you listen carefully to all the questions you are asked so that you can give clear concise responses. Make sure the interviewer has finished speaking before you begin to answer. General manners will go a long way in an interview as you need to have the 'likability' factor as well as the skills required to fulfil the job role.

EXAMPLE QUESTIONS AND HOW TO ANSWER THEM

The following questions are ones that you must be prepared for. The majority of them will crop up in your interview and it's important to answer them confidently and well by turning any negative into a positive. Firstly, you'll see a description of each question and how to answer them followed by the same table but this time filled with example answers:

What do you know about this company?

> It is essential to do your research on any organisation or employer that you apply for. Aside from it showing good preparation, it shows you care about the job you are applying for. If you know nothing about them you may as well go home as you won't be getting the job. Learn what games they have made previously, how long they have existed as a company, what platforms they develop for. How big the company is etc.

Tell me about yourself?

> This part can be tricky for some. It's important to have a lot to say but don't waffle on about things your interviewer has no care for. He/she doesn't need to know Jo Bloggs is your favourite footballer or that you managed to down a pint in under 10 seconds. Keep it relevant. Talk about your passion for games and what/how you've set your career path into becoming a game designer.

Are you currently employed?

> Show off here. If you are employed tell them your qualities that you offer in your current role and how it's developed you as a person. It's a good idea to mention any voluntary work, especially if it's related

to video games. If you're not currently employed then describe how you are doing voluntary work – as you should be! And that you've had a great opportunity to work on your portfolio and develop your skills. If you've just come out of University describe how passionate and driven you are to now succeed.

What do you think the most challenging aspect of this job will be for you?

This question is trying to be negative so it's very important for you to change that and make a positive from it. It could be adjusting to the companies workflow but you're very flexible and a quick learner.

What are the qualities you believe you bring to this job?

You must say how much you want to be a part of the games industry – it is your dream job and this provides huge drive. Take this opportunity to list the qualities that the company listed in its job description and provide your own examples from previous jobs and experiences to back it up.

What is your biggest strength?

Again, like before, show you have a drive for success. Tell them what your strengths are and how they have come of use in the past. Provide real life examples.

What is your biggest weakness?

Again turn any weakness you give into something positive. You lack experience…however this motivates you to progress.

How do you think your previous work colleagues would describe you?

Mention only positives here. It's a good idea to show that you are honest and reliable. If you are the type of person who lifts the team up say so etc.

Describe to me a time where you worked effectively as part of a team.

Think back to a time where someone you worked with was in need of help or where you were placed in a position of responsibility amongst your colleagues.

Where do you see yourself in 5 years time?

You can answer this question cleverly by saying that you hope you're still in the role you're applying for today and that your ideal scenario is that your colleagues and people in general are discussing and appreciating your work and design input as that is a very rewarding feeling for someone in this creative industry.

Do you have any questions for me?

It is essential you have at least one question to ask in the interview. There are a few you can learn which I will describe later but also try and pick up on some of the things the interviewer has said and ask questions about them. For instance they may have earlier described what team you will be working with, you could ask how many people are in the team or who's the team lead. Don't ask questions about taking a holiday or a pay rise already!

When answering interview questions try your best to be confident, remember they are not professional interviewers. Tell them qualities about yourself that match those in the job description that the company posted and provide your own examples from previous jobs and experiences to back up your qualities.

Working in the game industry is your dream job.

Below is the same table again but this time with example answers to the questions. You may take bits of inspiration from these examples for your own interview however you must make your interview your own and tailored to your own experiences and qualities.

What do you know about this company?

I know that since forming in 2002 this company has worked on many games for the mobile platform and has had success with many titles and is expanding in scale and recognition within the industry and I hope it is something I can be a part of as I feel it's an exciting time for this company and the game industry.

Tell me about yourself?

Working within the game industry is my dream job. Ever since playing my first game as a child I knew I wanted to be designing them. I set my academic path to support this and remain an active user in the online communities and modding forums for games. When I play games at home I am always analysing them to see how things are put together. One of my hobbies is photography; I carry my camera everywhere and often find myself taking pictures of the floor or walls in public to get a texture for my collection!

Are you currently employed?

> *I have just completed my university degree but have been doing voluntary work for independent game teams whilst at university which I have continued. While looking for the right game design job, I have been working part time in retail and this has allowed me to really build up my skills and portfolio. I've got such a huge drive to succeed and show off what I can do.*

What do you think the most challenging aspect of this job will be for you?

> *I would say that my biggest challenge may be learning any proprietary software or adjusting to the workflow that the company has but I am young, a quick learner and flexible so I know it won't be a problem.*

What are the qualities you believe you bring to this job?

> *I have great communication skills, I like to make sure I know everyone I'm working with and I feel I get on with anyone. I'm good at working to deadlines, always creating action plans and to do lists. In my previous job I had to complete my duties in half the normal time so I created a quick list and prioritised the most important tasks and how long it'd take me to complete them. I've great attention to detail and love puzzle solving – a lot of my games that I play are puzzle based games.*

What is your biggest strength?

> *My biggest strength is probably my determination to succeed. I want my work to be of the highest standard possible and I look back and feel I*

how2become

achieved the best I could in a project. I'm very committed and focused which can be seen in my portfolio work as I set out to create this particular piece within a month and I finished it in three weeks and used that extra time to get feedback from others and polish it even further.

What is your biggest weakness?

Because I have not long graduated from university I do have a lack of experience but this only motivates me to get a job and do well more. I am keen to progress.

How do you think your previous work colleagues would describe you?

I think that they would say I am bubbly and a happy person. I hope they would regard me as someone who is honest, trustworthy and a hard worker.

Describe to me a time where you worked effectively as part of a team.

One time when working in retail the manager, who locks up at the end of the day, feel ill and she had to leave work unexpectedly. I got the team together and we all took on and coordinated the tasks the manager had yet to finish. I called up the head office to find out what I had to do to lock up the shop at the end of the day.

Where do you see yourself in 5 years time?

I hope that in five years time I will be still doing this role I am applying for today and that my colleagues appreciate my work. It's something I find very rewarding as a creative person when someone, even

*random people on a forum may talk a part of a game
I helped develop and pay it a compliment.*

Do you have any questions for me?

*I do. What is the work environment like here? You
mentioned earlier that the team I'll be working with
is quite small, how many other people are on my
team? What software do you use in development?*

Now it is your chance to fill in the questions as a rough
template to how you'd answer these questions in your
interview:

What do you know about this company?

Tell me about yourself?

Are you currently employed?

What do you think the most challenging aspect of this job will be for you?

What are the qualities you believe you bring to this job?

What is your biggest strength?

What is your biggest weakness?

How do you think your previous work colleagues would describe you?

Describe to me a time where you worked effectively as part of a team.

Where do you see yourself in 5 years time?

Do you have any questions for me?

CHAPTER NINE

TOP TEN INSIDER TIPS

1. **Making contacts.** You know that old saying 'It's not what you know, it's who you know'? Well it may not be 100% true but there certainly is truth in it. Make sure, whatever your stage in life that you are being social, always demonstrating you're a hard worker to those around you. You'll find that people on your University course or colleges at an unrelated job will mostly likely at one point or another know of someone or something related to your speciality, and if you've shown passion and friendliness towards them they'll mostly think of you when an opportunity comes along.

2. **Have a portfolio you're confident in.** Your past work and portfolio play a huge part in getting a job within the games industry so make sure you show your reviewer what you are capable of.

- If you're in doubt leave it out of your portfolio. Your portfolio will only be as good as your worst bit of work in it.

- If you are not confident in your own work, it shows.

- Have a varied portfolio. Don't make your work tie you down to specific games. E.g. don't get the developer thinking "this person can only make racing games as all they have are cars in their showreel".

- If your online work takes a long time to load then you will lose a potential employer's interest immediately. Avoid flash based websites and fancy transitions to get around this.

- Not everyone will have the same taste of music as you so be careful what you chose for your showreel, dubsteb may not be the right choice.

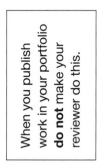

When you publish work in your portfolio **do not** make your reviewer do this.

3. **Learn from your mistakes.** Do not be afraid of making mistakes. Everyone makes mistakes and no one gets everything right the first time. This is important to remember as your career will be one big learning process and you will be given the same work back again and again to do more than once. Don't see this as a negative, it is the only way you can improve your work and become better at what you do. It is also very important to always have a willingness to learn. A development studio doesn't want to hear "that can't be done". You're in a creative industry were technology is

advancing all the time, contribute to that advancement.

4. **Get inspiration from everywhere.** Playing games is good and essential for a game industry job but you should be finding inspiration for your creativity in other places too. Books, history, museums are some great places to look. Even other peoples work but never plagiarise! Ever.

5. **Preparation is key.** Good preparation is essential for the getting a job, especially interviews. Practice example questions and repeat them aloud. Speaking them can help prevent you from becoming tongue tied in the actual interview. And remember you are being interviewed by a professional game designer not a professional interviewer!

6. **Research.** You should conduct research for your job role, the industry structure, your portfolio, your CV, your interview – every aspect and stage of becoming a game designer. It's important to be knowledgeable of not only the tools and software required for your job role but also the pipeline and the day-to-day basis routine of that role. Always research each company you apply for, especially before an interview and find out its history and its own structure then demonstrate this knowledge in your interview to really impress them.

7. **Get feedback.** You are never going to be able to grow as a developer if you don't take criticism onboard and strive to improve yourself. With any work you do you should try to ask for people's opinions and find ways to improve it. Online forums are a fantastic way to do this as you'll often find the industry's best developers online posting on forums and even on your posts providing expert advice and best of all – its free advice!

8. **Don't give up.** Sometimes there will be situations where becoming a game designer seems like a long way off or getting a job will never happen. It will. Be persistent and every second you are unemployed work on your portfolio and improving your skills. Your break will come but you will have to work for it and present yourself in an employable manner like those suggested in the CV, Portfolio and Interview chapters of this book.

9. **Have a passion for games.** If you aren't an avid gamer or you dislike games then the games industry is not the right industry for you. Most job adverts will list a passion for gaming as a requirement. It can be a demanding industry so that passion for games will often be carrying you through the 'crunch' times. Make sure you play a variety of games too and aside from having fun, think 'how did the developers make this part'.

10. **Make games.** In your spare time when you are not job hunting you should be making games, either as a personal project or a group project with people in a similar situation as you. Make simple games in *Adobe Flash* or work in a team and aim for something bigger in *Crytek's CryEngine*. The choice is yours. The experiences you can gain from this are great and well worth your investment in time as it can lead to you being able to add new content to your portfolio, CV and a more experienced you.

CHAPTER TEN

HOW TO BECOME A FREELANCE GAME DESIGNER

Traditionally a freelancer would be thought of as a writer, journalist or novelist. However, times have quickly moved on and in this digital age freelancers can be found in most sectors within the game industry. A freelance writer is still very important and many game studios hire a writer on a short contract for scripting and dialogue and even the game design document. Freelance animators, artists and audio workers are widely used too.

Freelance game designers at the very top of their field can earn around thirty pounds an hour. Typically, a freelance programmer will earn the most.

So, there are jobs available, you get to work remotely at home as and when you choose plus you get to work on lots of different projects often resulting in lots of variation of work and increasing your portfolio's depth and variety. Sounds

great right? Well it is for some but it does have its fair share of drawbacks. One of the biggest drawbacks being there is no job security. You may have work for a month or two and then suddenly nothing. Many people can find this hard, especially when they have bills to pay regularly but no regular income. Aside from this factor freelancing is a tough business to be in. It's a common thought that freelancers will spend more time looking for work than actually doing work. This isn't so true once you've been doing it for a while and built up a client list but starting up can be very tricky.

FINDING FREELANCE WORK

Similar to what the Networking chapter of this book teaches, you will once again find a great, and probably the best way to getting consistent work, is to gain contacts by networking. Go to parties, industry meet ups (GameDev, Meetup.com, E3 Expo etc.), let family and friends know you are freelancing create a LinkedIn account and visit groups and advertise yourself on online forums by being an active member.

When using an online forum **use your 'signature' for each message you post as an advert for your expertise.** Use it to let people know what you specialise in, a portfolio link and that you are a freelance worker.

The Bidding Process
Bid = Top Hours * Top Rate * Potential Errors

Once you have found a client you will typically receive an email from them asking how much you charge. This question can be difficult; almost annoying at times as you will mostly have to reply with "That depends". It will depend on the quality, quantity and type of work they are after. However, try to give them a number in your first email response as they will have a figure in their head that they are comparing you to other freelancers out there.

Knowing what to charge can be tough but a great strategy is to present a figure (your bid) in a best and worst case scenario. For example if they ask a freelance audio artist to create sound effects for a 30 second cut scene you may bid £30 best-case but in case it requires bits adding and tweaking later on with different game directions, £40.

QUOTES/CONTRACTS

When discussing a contract with a client make sure you are very professional, do what you say you can/will do and present yourself in a clear manner. Make sure they know what they are paying for. There are generally two ways to offer your work; in a pay per asset (i.e. a sound effect/3D model/cut-scene etc.) or a pay per time (i.e. a week/month/year). For larger scale games it may be preferable to work on a per-month or per-project basis as opposed to per asset. This is because it will then not be about trying to create as many assets as possible in a short space of time but rather it'll be about producing your best quality work.

Sometimes you will under quote yourself and find that tasks will be harder to complete or need more work. If the

scope does dramatically change that your working hours are impacted seriously then draw up a new contract that details any new work, so that there won't be any shocks to your employer. It's a good way of letting them know during the development process that if more work is asked for it will affect the invoice at the end. It's always best to stay to the original quote you provided as much as you possibly can. Your client will appreciate your hard work and hopefully offer or refer you to more work in the future.

Be Professional and don't be that person who puts their creativity above professionalism. Make sure to use correct spelling, grammar and no use of short-hand in your emails. Respond promptly and be friendly and courteous. Being consistently professional will put you head and shoulders above the competition.

TIPS TO REMEMBER AS A FREELANCE GAME DESIGNER

- **It's not your game** – You must always create the client's game, not your own! Sometimes you will feel like you have a better idea but if your client doesn't want it you a duty to execute your client's wishes and vision, not your own.

- **Build a Reputation** – Whether you intend to or not you will be building up a reputation simply by working and communicating. Your reputation will carry you as

a freelance worker. This means it's important to ensure you are regarded as trustworthy – don't disrespect your client by saying bad things about them and don't spill the beans on their project. Your client will hopefully refer you to other work in the future but they will not do this if your work and you yourself are not professional.

- **Know your limits** – You need to know your limits as a freelancer. Don't take on too much and space out what you do take on. Roughly 20 hours a week should be set aside for freelance work with any client, not much more. This is because you will need time to work on any problems, the flexibility for important rush jobs.

- **Deliver what you agreed** – Stand by your original contract and deliver what you promised: timeframe, budget, content etc. Do your best to overcome problems without affecting the original agreement but in the worst case scenario inform your client as soon as possible to let them know there is a problem that will affect your contract's original agreement.

- **Respect confidentiality agreements** – Many developers, even independent ones will require you to sign a confidentiality agreement before you start working with them. Your hard earned reputation will be in tatters if you break it! It's worth noting that even if the information you have spoken about was already leaked by another employer you will still be in breach of your agreement.

- **You are always networking** – Whoever you deal with, you will be networking and potentially, if they like you, opening future doors for job opportunity.

- **Be active online** – Use online creative communities to advertise yourself, be an active contributor and show

off your work. Make sure you let them know you are a freelancer. You can do this on every single post by stating it in your forum signature. You will of course have a website for your online portfolio but create a blog too and if you want to really draw in the attention create tutorials or post helpful articles for others.

- **Contracts are not money in the bank** – Contracts are very important but they are not money. Any work that will pay out over £300 take a 25% down payment.

- **Don't be afraid to work outside the game industry** – You won't always be finding jobs that involve making assets for games so a good way to keep up the income is to find freelance work in other creative industries, media, design, adverting etc. www.elance.com and www.odesk.com are great places for this.

CHAPTER ELEVEN

STARTING YOUR OWN
INDEPENDENT COMPANY

THE LEGAL STUFF

If you are considering entering the game industry with your own independent company (also known as an 'indie company') then be warned, it is a tough process that needs thorough research. Many people are going down this road and what starts out as a group of friends building a game and connecting through Skype turns into an official company with official employees. Below are some of the basic areas and tips you should consider:

Becoming Official – Registering Your Company

Setting yourself up as the sole-trader is very advisable as it has the lowest start-up cost and hence is the lowest risk-to-profit strategy. It's relatively easy to register yourself, and in England and Wales this can even be done online through the

government website at www.companieshouse.gov.uk.

You will probably be charged business rates, which are essentially taxes for using property for business purposes (England and Wales). You have to handle your own tax assessment and ensure all owed VAT is accounted and paid for. This is very important – you can get into serious trouble for not paying owed tax!

Protecting Your Work – Copyright

The UK has a strong tradition of intellectual property rights and all works will be protected automatically. This includes material uploaded to the internet. However, it is surprisingly easy to sign these rights away. Hidden within the lengthy terms and conditions of many popular websites such as *Facebook*, *Twitter* and *Instagram* are clauses which state that they have full permission to use your material. If you want to upload material to the internet, try to keep the bulk of your work on websites you know to be safe, preferably on one with an address owned by you.

The government is very stringent with handing out patents, and it is not necessary to have one.

Avoiding Trademark Legal Issues

In order to avoid accidentally stealing a trademarked name or brand off another company do a check using www.ipo.gov.uk to view registered names. If someone else has chosen your desired name, then you have to choose another one. If your name is available, consider registering it but first it may be a good idea to discuss the idea with your lawyer. This is partially due to the misconception that registering a company at Companies House protects that name as a registered copyright. This is untrue.

It is a good idea to search for domain names that use the name you wish to use. If the intended .com is not available, someone else may already have used your name as a trader mark, perhaps as an unregistered trademark or one registered outside the UK. If your desired domain name is available, consider purchasing it and any other variants you can afford – .co.uk, .org, .net and so on. This will keep your path smooth for the future.

How to Expand Your Company

As a sole trader you are allowed to take the usual steps to expanding your business, such as hiring employees. However, since serious taxes start kicking in after earning 35k in revenue, it is advisable to change to a limited company. This separates your company's finances with your personal finances, which is a great help as your business expands. Again, this can be done at Companies House and is a relatively straightforward process.

Outsourcing work is something you should seriously consider. This means that instead of going through the massive expense of hiring employees, you can send one off jobs to people with the skills to complete it effectively. For example, if you want host your own game website, you can ask a company like Kenmore Design to create one for you. This is usually a cheaper way of effectively getting jobs completed.

Bank Account Trick

As a sole trader you you company's finances and your own are indistinguishable. All debts your company racks up will affect your own finances. Until you are ready to become a limited company, creating a new bank account specifically for your company's finances makes it easier to manage and track your money.

Raising Finance

Due to current government policies to help small businesses, you may wish to consider the Seed Enterprise Investment Scheme. This is a tax incentive designed to help small businesses by encouraging individuals to invest in them, including friends and family. It generously offers income tax relief at a rate of 50per cent of the invested amount, irrespective of the rate of income tax the investor is subject to. The maximum amount of money that can be invested in a company via this scheme is an also generous amount of £150,000.

12 COMMON THINGS YOU SHOULD AIM TO DO AS AN INDEPENDENT DEVELOPER

Start small. The new *Call of Duty* may be overly ambitious for you to make, but the new *Angry Birds* is not. By focusing on the smaller, manageable, high reward games you can build up your business and knowledge.

Have a plan. Get that end object in mind and dig paths to get to it. Planning will make your work more efficient and safer, with fewer issues later on.

Work together. Absolutely everyone needs help. Bouncing ideas and asking advice off others will go a long way to help you. You will likely find most fellow independent designers to be friendly and should be happy to help and talk ideas with you.

Embrace wacky concepts. Unique game titles are often the most successful, and you should be using your strengths as an independent developer to pursue these concepts unconstrained. At the same time, don't feel too forced to embrace wacky concepts. You are independent because

you are unconstrained. Many independent studios create traditional style games with great success.

Keep up your passion. Whilst you have to be practical to the point of ruthlessness, being passionate strongly affects your work in a positive way. Let this passion motivate your employees and create a joint vision.

Have perspective. Know your work for both its faults and its virtues. Through this, you can iron out the problems within your projects.

Make great artwork. This is the first thing people will see and so is vital. Make great artwork, a unique art style or at least style and consistency if you struggle with the art side.

Take advantage of all relevant areas. PR, customer service, employee wellbeing – areas that may seem not to be about creating the perfect game but are nevertheless vital for success. Use forums to your advantage by taking in community feedback.

Keep independent! *Steam*, *Android* and the *iOS* until recently did not exist. Yet they have proven invaluable for many. Let your hands be untied so you can take full advantage of future opportunities.

Independent business should be one of peace, not war. As an independent designer, you have the ability, as do those you work with, to walk away from any bad deal, to say goodbye to an unpleasant businessman. You in turn have to be direct and pleasant yourself.

Build up the foundations to get to that dream game you have always wanted to make. Unravelling what makes "you" you – your taste, what you care about, your abilities – is a great pleasure of life and is symbiotic with being an independent creator.

CHAPTER TWELVE
CONCLUSION

By reaching the end of this guide you are ready to begin pursuing your career as a game designer and prepare for your application process. Now is a great time to enter the fast paced, exciting and challenging world of the video game industry. There are always companies and people looking for new talented game designers around the world. The successful one's who break into the industry quickest have strong self belief, prepare fully, persevere. There is no reason why you cannot have your dream job.

Thank you for purchasing and taking the time to read this book. I have greatly enjoyed writing it and I hope it helps you to achieve your goal in becoming a game designer. Good luck!

APPENDIX A

Bournemouth University

The Media School, W328 Weymouth House, Talbot Campus, Poole, BH12 5BB

- Engineering Doctorate/ Professional Doctorate (EngD/ ProfD) in Digital Media, 4 years full-time

www.digital-entertainment.org

Birmingham City University – Gamer Camp

NTI Birmingham, 15 Bartholomew Row, Birmingham, B5 5JU

- Gamer Camp: Pro (MA / MSc in Video Games Development, 1 Year)
- Gamer Camp: Nano (Short course, 1 month)

www.gamercamp.co.uk

Bournemouth University – National Centre for Computer Animation

Bournemouth Media School, Bournemouth University, Talbot Campus, Poole, BH12 5BB

- 3D Computer Animation (MA/MSc, 1 Years)
- Digital Effects (MA/MFA, 1 Years)
- Computer Animation (BA/BGA, 3 Years)

ncca.bournemouth.ac.uk

Brunel University – School of Arts

Brunel University, Uxbridge, Middlesex, UB8 3PH

- MA Digital Games: Theory & Design (MA/MFA and BA Digital Games [Joint Honours only], 1 Year)

brunel.ac.uk/about/acad/sa/artsub/filmtv/videogames

City University London School of Informatics

Northampton Square, London EC1V 0HB

- BSc (Hons) Computer Science with Games Technology (BSc, 3 Years)
- MSc Computer Games Technology (MSc, 1 Year)

www.soi.city.ac.uk

De Montfort University

Faculty of Art and Design, Leicester, LE1 9BH

- Game Art Design (Certificate/Diploma)

www.dmu.ac.uk/faculties/art_and_design/ug_courses/game_art.jsp

Escape Studios

Shepherds West, Rockley Road, London, W14 0DA

www.escapestudios.com

Glamorgan Centre for Art & Design Technology

Glyntaff Road, Pontypridd, CF37 4AT

- Computer Animation (BA/BGA and BA [Hons], 3 Years)

www.gcadt.ac.uk

Glasgow Caledonian University

70 Cowcaddens Rd, Glasgow, G4 0BA

- BA 3D Computer Animation (4 Years)
- BA Computer Games (Art & Animation) (4 Years)
- BSc Computer Games (Design) (4 Years)

- BSc Computer Games (Software Development) (4 Years)
- BSc Audio Technology with Multimedia (4 Years)

www.gcu.ac.uk

Glasgow Caledonian University, School of Engineering and Computing Division of Computing and Creative Technologies

Cowcaddens Road, Glasgow, G4 0BA

- Computer Games (Software Developemnt) (BSc, 4 Years)
- Computer Games (Design) (BSc, 4 Years)

www.gcu.ac.uk/sec/study

Goldsmiths College, University of London, Department of Computing

New Cross, London, SE14 6NW

- MSc Computer Games & Entertainment (1 Year)

www.gamesgoldsmiths.com

International Centre for Digital Content – Liverpool John Moores University

Redmond Close, 20 St James Road, Liverpool L1 7BY

- Digital Games (MA/MFA, 1 Year)

www.icdc.org.uk/magames

Lancaster University UK

Infolab21, Lancaster, LA1 4WA

- Mobile Games Development (MA/MFA)

www.dcs.lancs.ac.uk/admissions/postgraduate_courses.php?course_id=008623

London College of Music and Media Creative Technologies Ctr

Grove House, The Grove, Ealing, London, W5 5DX

- Music Technology (BSc)

music.tvu.ac.uk/index.php

Middlesex University

The Burroughs, Hendon, London, NW4 4BT

- Computing, Graphics and Games (BSc, 3 Years)
- Interactive Systems Design (BSc, 3 Years)
- Multimedia Computing (BSc, 3 Years)
- Design For Interactive Media (MA/MFA, 1 Year)
- Animation (BA/BGA, 3 Years)
- 3D Animation and Games (BA/BGA, 3 Years)

www.mdx.ac.uk

Motherwell College

Dalzell Drive, Motherwell, ML1 2DD

- National Certificate/Diploma

www.motherwell.ac.uk

National Film and Television School

Beaconsfield Studios, Station Road, Beaconsfield, HP9 1LG

- MA Games Design and Development (MA/MFA, 2 Years)

www.nfts.co.uk/courses/games-design-and-development

National Centre for Computer Animation

Bournemouth University, Talbot Campus, Fern Barrow, Poole, BH12 5BB

ncca.bournemouth.ac.uk

Nescot
Reigate Road, Epsom, KT17 3DS
- First Diploma Game Development (Certificate/Diploma, 1 Year)
- National Diploma Game Development (Certificate/Diploma, 1 Year)

www.nescot.ac.uk

Northern Regional College
Ballymoney Campus, 2 Coleraine Road, Ballymoney, BT53 6BP
- Level 3 BTEC Extended Diploma in Creative Media Production (Games Development) (2 Years)

www.nrc.ac.uk

Northumbria University
Ellison Building, Ellison Place, Newcastle upon Tyne, NE1 8ST
- BSc Computer Games Software Engineering (BSc, 4 Years)
- MSc Computer Games Design and Production (BSc, 3 Years)

northumbria.ac.uk

Norwich University College of the Arts
Francis House, 3-7 Redwell Street, Norwich, NR2 4SN
- Games Art and Design (BA/BGA, 3 Years)

www.nuca.ac.uk

Queen's University Belfast
School of EEECS, Queen's University Belfast, University Road, Belfast, Antrim, BT7 1NN
- Computer Games Design and Development (MEng, 5 Years)

www.qub.ac.uk/eeecs

Ravensbourne College Of Design & Communication
Walden Rd, Chislehurst, BR7 5SN
- Computer Visualisation and Animation (BA/BGA and BA Hons, 2 Years)
- Animation (BA/BGA and BA Hons, 1 Years)
- Interactive Digital Media* (MA)

www.rave.ac.uk

School of Arts and Humanities
University Campus Suffolk, Waterfront Building, Neptune Quay, Ipswich, IP4 1QJ
- Computer Games Design (BA/BGA, 3 Years)

www.ucs.ac.uk

School of Computing and Intelligent Systems, Faculty of Computing and Engineering
University of Ulster, Northland Road, Derry, BT48 7JL
- BEng (Hons) Computer Games Development (BSc, 4 Years)
- BSc (Hons) Multimedia Computer Games (BSc, 4 Years)

www.ulster.ac.uk

Staffordshire University
Faculty of Computing, Engineering and Technology, Beaconside, Stafford, ST18 0AD
- Games Design (MSc, BSc and Beng Meng)
- Multiplayer Games Design (BSc and Beng Meng)
- Games Concepts Design (BSc, 3 Years)
- Portable Games Programming 3FT/4SW Hon BSc
- Multiplayer Online Games Programming (G621) 3FT/4FT Hon BEng
- Computer Games Programming 3FT/4SW Hon BSc

www.staffs.ac.uk

Stroud College in Gloucestershire
Stratford Road, Stroud, Gloucestershire, GL5 4AH
- Multimedia – BTEC National Diploma (Multimedia – BTEC National Diploma, 2 Years)

www.stroud.ac.uk

Swansea Metropolitan University – School of Digital Media
Mount Pleasant, Swansea, Swansea, SA1 6ED
- Creative Computer Games Design (PhD, MSc, BSc, BA/BGA, Computer Games Development and 3D Computer Animation, 3 Years)
- BSc(Hons) Computer Games Development
- BSc(Hons) 3D Computer Animation
- BA(Hons) 3D Computer Animation

www.smu.ac.uk

Train2Game
Nationwide, United Kingdom
- TIGA Diploma in Games Design (Certificate/Diploma, 1 Year)
- TIGA Diploma in Games Development (Certificate/ Diploma, 1 Year)

www.train2game.com

University for the Creative Arts at Farnham
Farnham Campus, Falkner Road, Farnham, GU9 7DS
- BA Computer Games Arts (BA/BGA)

www.ucreative.ac.u

University of Abertay Dundee
Bell Street, Dundee, Scotland, DD1 1HG
- Computer Games Technology (BSc, 4 Years)

- Computer Arts (BA/BGA, 4 Years)
- Computer Games Technology (MSc, 16 Months)
- Game Art & Animation (MA/MFA, 16 Months)
- Game Design & Production Management (BA/BGA, 4 Years)
- Creative Sound Production (BA/BGA, 2 Years)
- Computer Game Applications Development (BSc, 4 Years)
- Games Development (MProf, 1 Years)

www.abertay.ac.uk

University of Birmingham School of Computer Science
Birmingham, B15 2TT
Research programmes in:
- Artificial Intelligence (AI) & Cognitive Science
- Evolutionary & Neural Computation
- Human Computer Interaction (HCI)
- Image Understanding and Computer vision
- Mathematical foundations of Computer Science & Programming languages
- Modelling and Analysis of systems
- Networks and Communications
- Robotics

www.cs.bham.ac.uk

University of Bradford – School of Informatics
Richmond Road, Bradford, BD7 1DP
- Interactive Systems and Video Games Design (BSc, 3 Years)
- Design for Computer Games (BA/BGA, 3 Years)
- Artificial Intelligence for Games (MSc)

www.inf.brad.ac.uk

University of Glamorgan
- Treforest, Pontypridd, CF37 1DL
- Computer Game Development (BSc)

www.glam.ac.uk

University of Hull – Department of Computer Science

Department of Computer Science, University of Hull,
Hull,HU6 7RX
- Games Programming (MSc and BSc)

www.net.dcs.hull.ac.uk

University of Lincoln

Brayford Pool, Lincoln, LN6 7TS
- Games Computing (BSc)
- Advanced Games Programming (MSc)

www.lincoln.ac.uk/dci

University of Portsmouth – School of Creative Technologies

Eldon Building, Winston Churchill Road, Portsmouth, PO1
2DJ
- Computer Games Technology (MSc and BSc, 3 Years)

www.port.ac.uk/games

University of Sheffield

Department of Computer Science, Regent Court, 211
Portobello St, Sheffield, S1 4DP
- Computer Science (MA/MFA and BA/BGA)

www.dcs.shef.ac.uk

University of Wales, Newport

Allt-yr-yn Campus, PO Box 180, Newport, NP20 5DA
- Animation (BA (Hons), 3 Years)

- Games Development and Artificial Intelligence (BSc (Hons), 3 Years)
- Computer Games Design (BA (Hons), 3 Years)

www.newport.ac.uk

University of Teesside School of Computing and Mathematics
Middlesbrough, Cleveland, TS1 3BA

- Computer Games Design (MA/MFA, BSc, BA/BGA and HND / BSc / BA / MSc / MA)
- Interactive Computer Entertainment (MA/MFA, BSc, BA/BGA and HND / BSc / BA / MSc / MA)
- Visualisation (BSc, BA/BGA, MA/MFA and HND / BSc / BA / MSc / MA)
- Computer Games Art (MA/MFA, BSc, BA/BGA and HND / BSc / BA / MSc / MA)
- Computer Animation (MA/MFA, BSc, BA/BGA and HND / BSc / BA / MSc / MA)
- Virtual Reality (MA/MFA, BSc, BA/BGA and HND / BSc / BA / MSc / MA)

www-scm.tees.ac.uk/html/undergraduate_computer_ games_courses.html

Anglia Ruskin University
Bishop Hall Lane, Chelmsford, Essex, CM1 1SQ

- Computer Games and Visual Effects
- 3 year full-time Degree

tel: 44 (0) 845 271 3333
www.anglia.ac.uk

University of Bolton
Deane Road, Bolton, BL3 5AB

- Computer Games Software Development, 3 year full-time Degree

- Games Art (GH46) 3FT Hon BA
- Games Design (24WG) 2FT HND
- Games Design (G613) 3FT Hon BSc

www.bolton.ac.uk

Glyndwr University

Plas Coch, Mold Road, Wrexham, LL11 2AW

- Computer Game Development, 3 year full-time Degree
- Design: Creative Media 3FT Hon BA Hons

www.glyndwr.ac.uk

University of Hertfordshire

College Lane, Hatfield, Herts, AL10 9AB

- 3D Games Art (3 year full-time Degree)

www.herts.ac.uk

The University of Hull

Cottingham Road, Hull, HU6 7RX

- Computer Science with Games Development (G490) 3FT Hon BSc
- Computer Science with Games Development 4FT Hon Meng

www.hull.ac.uk

Hull College

Queen's Gardens, Hull, HU1 3DG

- Games Design, 3 year full-time Degree

tel: 44 (0) 1482 329943
www.hull-college.ac.uk/HE

Kingston University

Cooper House, 40-46 Surbiton Road, Kingston upon
Thames, KT1 2HX
- Games Technology, 3 year full-time Degree

tel: (0) 844 8552177
www.kingston.ac.uk

Leeds Metropolitan University

City Site, Leeds, LS1 3HE
- Games Design (3 year full-time Degree, 4 year
  sandwich Degree)

www.leedsmet.ac.uk

University of Lincoln

Brayford Pool, Lincoln, LN6 7TS
- Computer Games Production, 3 year full-time Degree, 4
  year sandwich Degree (G612)
- 4FT/5SW Hon/Deg Mcomp / BsC Games Computing
  (G401)
- 3FT/4SW Hon BSc, (G610)
- 4FT/5SW Hon/Deg

www.lincoln.ac.uk

Newcastle College

Rye Hill Campus, Scotswood Road, Newcastle upon Tyne,
NE4 7SA
- Computing for Games and Interactive Media 2 year full-
  time Foundation Degree
- Games Development (WG2K) 2FT Fdg FdSc

www.newcastlecollege.co.uk

Northbrook College Sussex
Littlehampton Road, Goring by Sea, Worthing, West Sussex
BN12 6NU
- Computing (Games Design) 2 year full-time Foundation Degree

www.northbrook.ac.uk

University of Plymouth
Drake Circus, Plymouth, PL4 8AA
- Computing and Games Development 3 year full-time Degree, 4 year sandwich Degree

www.plymouth.ac.uk

Southampton Solent University
East Park Terrace, Southampton, Hampshire, SO14 0RT
- Computer and Video Games, 3 year full-time Degree
- Computer and Video Games (G450) 3FT Hon BA
- Computer Games Development 3FT Hon BSc (G615) 4SW Hon BSc (G616) 4FT Hon BSc

www.solent.ac.uk

St Helens College
Water Street, St Helens, Merseyside WA10 1PP
- Game Art 3 year full-time Degree

www.sthelens.ac.uk

Aberystwyth University
Penglais Campus, Aberystwyth, Ceredigion SY23 3FB
- Computer Graphics, Vision and Games 3 year full-time Degree
- Comp Graphics, Vision and Games (inc training) 4SW Hon BSc

tel: 44 (0) 1970 622021
www.aber.ac.uk

Blackpool and The Fylde College
Ashfield Road, Bispham, Blackpool, Lancs, FY2 0HB
- Game Design and Development 2 year full-time Foundation Degree

www.blackpool.ac.uk

Farnborough College of Technology
Boundary Road, Farnborough, Hampshire, GU14 6SB
- Computing with Gaming 3 year full-time Degree

www.farn-ct.ac.uk

Northbrook College Sussex
Littlehampton Road, Goring by Sea, Worthing West Sussex, BN12 6NU
- Computing (Games Design) 2 year full-time Foundation Degree

www.northbrook.ac.uk

Sheffield Hallam University
City Campus, Howard Street, Sheffield, S1 1WB
- Games Software Development, 4 year sandwich Degree 4FT/5SW Hon Mcomp

www.shu.ac.uk

South Nottingham College
West Bridgford Centre, Greythorn Drive, West Bridgford, Nottingham, NG2 7GA
- Computer Games and Interactive Media (Arts) 2 year full-time Foundation Degree

www.snc.ac.uk

University of Wolverhampton
MX207, Camp Street, Wolverhampton, WV1 1AD

- Computer Games Design, 3 year full-time Degree, 4 year sandwich Degree

www.wlv.ac.uk

University of the West of England, Bristol

Frenchay Campus, Coldharbour Lane, Bristol, BS16 1QY

- Computer Science for Games, 3 year full-time Degree, 4 year sandwich Degree

Games Technology (G611) 3FT/4SW Hon BSc

www.uwe.ac.uk

Chichester College

Westgate Fields, Chichester, West Sussex, PO19 1SB

- Computing, 2 year full-time HND

www.chichester.ac.uk

University of Greenwich

Old Royal Naval College, Park Row, London, SE10 9LS

- Games Technology, 3 year full-time Degree Fhert

www.gre.ac.uk

University of the Arts London

272 High Holborn, London, WC1V 7EY

- Games Design (W283) 2FT Fdg FdA
- Interactive Games Design (Top-Up) 1FT Hon BA

www.arts.ac.uk

University of Sussex

Sussex House, Brighton, BN1 9RH

- Games and Multimedia Environments, 3 year full-time Degree

www.sussex.ac.uk

The Manchester Metropolitan University
All Saints, Manchester, M15 6BH
- Computer Games Technology (Foundation) 4 year full-time Degree, 5 year sandwich Degree

www.mmu.ac.uk

The University of Gloucestershire
Waterworth Building, Park Campus, The Park, Cheltenham, GL50 2RH
- Interactive Games Design, 3 year full-time Degree, 4 year sandwich Degree

www.glos.ac.uk

University of Cumbria
Fusehill Street, Carlisle, Cumbria, CA1 2HH
- Art of Games Design, 2 year full-time Foundation Degree

www.cumbria.ac.uk

The University of Salford
Salford, M5 4WT
- Computer and Video Games, 3 year full-time Degree

www.salford.ac.uk

University of West London (formerly Thames Valley University)
St Mary's Road, Ealing, London, W5 5RF
- Games Development (Games Art, Games Design) 3 year full-time Degree

www.uwl.ac.uk

Bangor University
Bangor, Gwynedd, LL57 2DG

- Creative Technologies, 3 year full-time Degree

www.bangor.ac.uk

University of Glamorgan, Cardiff and Pontypridd
Enquiries and Admissions Unit, Pontypridd, CF37 1DL
- Computer Animation, 3 year full-time Degree

www.glam.ac.uk

London South Bank University
103 Borough Road, London, SE1 0AA
- Games Culture, 3 year full-time Degree

www.lsbu.ac.uk

Accrington & Rossendale College
Broad Oak Road, Accrington, Lancashire, BB5 2AW
- Computing, 2 year full-time Foundation Degree

www.accrosshighereducation.co.uk

Bradford College
Great Horton Road, Bradford, West Yorkshire, BD7 1AY
- Games Development, 3 year full-time Degree

www.bradfordcollege.ac.uk/university-centre

North East Worcestershire College
Peakman Street, Redditch, Worcestershire, B98 8DW
- Interactive Media and Games Development, 2 year full-time Foundation Degree

www.ne-worcs.ac.uk

University of Sunderland
The Student Gateway, Chester Road, Sunderland, SR1 3SD
- Games Software Development, 3 year full-time Degree, 4 year sandwich Degree

www.sunderland.ac.uk

University of Ulster
Coleraine, Co. Londonderry, Northern Ireland, BT52 1SA
- Computer Games Development, 4 year sandwich Degree

www.ulster.ac.uk

University of the West of Scotland
Paisley, Renfrewshire, Scotland, PA1 2BE
- Computer Animation with Games Development, 4 year full-time Degree, 3 year full-time Degree
- Computer Games Development (G610) 3FT/5SW Ord/ Hon BSc
- Computer Games Technology 3FT/4FT/5SW Ord/Hon BSc

www.uws.ac.uk

. . . .

Attend a 1-Day
Game Designer Course at:
www.GameDesignerCourses.com

. . . .